D0593677

University
of Michigan
Business
School Management Series

INNOVATIVE SOLUTIONS TO THE
PRESSING PROBLEMS OF BUSINESS

The mission of the University of Michigan Business School Management Series is to provide accessible, practical, and cutting-edge solutions to the most critical challenges facing businesspeople today. The UMBS Management Series provides concepts and tools for people who seek to make a significant difference in their organizations. Drawing on the research and experience of faculty at the University of Michigan Business School, the books are written to stretch thinking while providing practical, focused, and innovative solutions to the pressing problems of business.

Also available in the UMBS series:

Becoming a Better Value Creator, by Anjan V. Thakor

Achieving Success Through Social Capital, by Wayne Baker

Improving Customer Satisfaction, Loyalty, and Profit,
by Michael D. Johnson and Anders Gustafsson

The Compensation Solution, by John E. Tropman

Strategic Interviewing, by Richaurd Camp, Mary Vielhaber,
and Jack L. Simonetti

Creating the Multicultural Organization, by Taylor Cox

Getting Results, by Clinton O. Longenecker and
Jack L. Simonetti

A Company of Leaders, by Gretchen M. Spreitzer and
Robert E. Quinn

Managing the Unexpected, by Karl Weick and Kathleen Sutcliffe

Using the Law for Competitive Advantage, by George J. Siedel

For additional information on any of these titles or future
titles in the series, visit www.umbsbooks.com.

Executive Summary

Creativity has always been an essential way for organizations to make progress and, in turn, create value for stakeholders inside and outside the organization. The focus of creativity may be innovation in the traditional sense—the invention of outstanding products and services—but it may also be the development of new processes, new ways of communicating with customers, or new ways of attracting and retaining the best talent. Creativity as a core competence can help a company create products, services, processes, or ideas that are better or new.

Unfortunately, many companies and managers try to adopt a one-size-fits-all "best practice" for creativity, usually with disappointing results. The reason that these efforts fail is that each new endeavor needs a different approach to creativity. Your "best practices" and competencies will be different depending on what you need to achieve in your particular situation.

This book provides a comprehensive map of creativity at work that will help you recognize your creative situation and act accordingly. With this systematic approach, you can diagnose and assess what practices will work best for your circumstances. We provide examples from a variety of firms and tools that meet the requirements of each type of situation. Whether you are a top executive steering your firm or a manager responsible for a single unit, this book is for you.

Chapter One defines creativity and introduces the four major types of creativity on our map, which we characterize as profiles: Imagine, Invest, Improve, and Incubate. Each profile is best suited to certain kinds of business purposes, and each has its own distinctive practices. Furthermore, the four profiles can help you understand the creative preferences of organizations, departments, work groups, and individuals.

The creativity map helps you locate your current profile, understand where you need to go, and navigate toward your purposes. To achieve specific purposes, you have to use the right practices, and to accomplish the right practices, you need the right people. Chapter Two explains how to diagnose your situation and assess where you are with respect to creativity. Two main dimensions shape each profile: *focus* (internal versus external) and *approach* (divergent versus convergent). The combination of these dimensions produces two secondary dimensions of creativity: *magnitude* (big versus small) and *speed* (fast versus slow). The chapter ends with an assessment that allows you to identify and compare the profiles that describe your purposes, practices, and people.

The four core chapters of the book take an in-depth look at specific creativity practices for each profile. Imagine practices (Chapter Three), such as jump-starting and forecasting, are externally focused and produce big, breakthrough results by taking a divergent approach. Invest practices (Chapter Four), such as partnering or portfolios, are externally focused, yet they produce results quickly by taking a convergent approach. Improve practices (Chapter Five), such as modular design and development or process improvement systems, are focused on internal capabilities and produce smaller, incremental results with a convergent approach. Incubate practices (Chapter Six), such as talent scouting and idea spaces, are internally focused and tend to produce long-term results at a slower pace but allow a divergent approach to solutions.

Chapter Seven addresses how to blend creativity practices to meet the complex needs that characterize most work situations. The chapter discusses three steps for managing these different needs: set your direction, create an action plan to integrate the creativity practices that are appropriate to your situation, and develop the required creative abilities in your team and in yourself.

We suggest that the real art of creativity management and leadership is in blending the four profiles. After reviewing your personal and organizational creativity profiles, you will be capable of encouraging appropriate creativity in yourself and in others. No matter what your level of responsibility, you can use the creativity map to guide, manage, and integrate creativity practices within your organization, division, department, or team. Together you can move purposefully toward creating future value.

Creativity at Work

Developing the
Right Practices to
Make Innovation Happen

Jeff DeGraff
and Katherine A. Lawrence

JOSSEY-BASS
A Wiley Company
www.josseybass.com

Published by

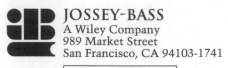

JOSSEY-BASS
A Wiley Company
989 Market Street
San Francisco, CA 94103-1741

www.josseybass.com

Copyright © 2002 by John Wiley & Sons, Inc.

Jossey-Bass is a registered trademark of John Wiley & Sons, Inc.

No part of this publication may be reproduced, stored in a retrieval system, or trans-
mitted in any form or by any means, electronic, mechanical, photocopying, recording,
scanning, or otherwise, except as permitted under Sections 107 or 108 of the 1976
United States Copyright Act, without either the prior written permission of the Publisher or authorization through payment of the appropriate per-copy fee to the Copyright Clearance Center, 222 Rosewood Drive, Danvers, MA 01923, (978) 750-8400, fax
(978) 750-4744. Requests to the Publisher for permission should be addressed to the
Permissions Department, John Wiley & Sons, Inc., 605 Third Avenue, New York, NY
10158-0012, (212) 850-6011, fax (212) 850-6008, e-mail: permreq@wiley.com.

Jossey-Bass books and products are available through most bookstores. To contact
Jossey-Bass directly, call (888) 378-2537, fax to (800) 605-2665, or visit our website
at www.josseybass.com.

Substantial discounts on bulk quantities of Jossey-Bass books are available to corporations, professional associations, and other organizations. For details and dis-
count information, contact the special sales department at Jossey-Bass.

We at Jossey-Bass strive to use the most environmentally sensitive paper stocks available to us. Our publications are printed on acid-free recycled stock whenever possible,
and our paper always meets or exceeds minimum GPO and EPA requirements.

Jossey-Bass also publishes its books in a variety of electronic formats. Some content
that appears in print may not be available in electronic books.

Library of Congress Cataloging-in-Publication Data

DeGraff, Jeff.
    Creativity at work: developing the right practices to make innovation
  happen/Jeff DeGraff and Katherine A. Lawrence.—1st. ed.
       p. cm.—(University of Michigan Business School management series)
  Includes bibliographical references and index.
  ISBN 0-7879-5725-9 (alk. paper)
    1. Organizational change. 2. Organizational effectiveness.
3. Creative ability in business. I. Lawrence, Katherine A., date.
II. Title. III. Series.

HD58.8 .D438 2002
658.4'063—dc21

2002005663

FIRST EDITION
HB Printing 10 9 8 7 6 5 4 3 2 1

Contents

Series Foreword

Welcome to the University of Michigan Business School Management Series. The books in this series address the most urgent problems facing business today. The series is part of a larger initiative at The University of Michigan Business School (UMBS) that ties together a range of efforts to create and share knowledge through conferences, survey research, interactive and distance training, print publications, and new media

It is just this type of broad-based initiative that sparked my love affair with UMBS in 1984. From the day I arrived I was enamored with the quality of the research, the quality of the MBA program, and the quality of the Executive Education Center. Here was a business school committed to new lines of research, new ways of teaching, and the practical application of ideas. It was a place where innovative thinking could result in tangible outcomes.

The UMBS Management Series is one very important outcome, and it has an interesting history. It turns out that every year five thousand participants in our executive program fill out a marketing survey in which they write statements indicating the most important problems they face. One day Lucy Chin, one of our administrators, handed me a document containing all these statements. A content analysis of the data resulted in a list of forty-five pressing problems. The topics ranged from growing a company to managing personal stress. The list covered a wide territory, and I started to see its potential. People in organizations tend to be driven by a very traditional set of problems, but the solutions evolve. I went to my friends at Jossey-Bass to discuss a publishing project. The discussion eventually grew into the University of Michigan Business School Management Series— Innovative Solutions to the Pressing Problems of Business.

The books are independent of each other, but collectively they create a comprehensive set of management tools that cut across all the functional areas of business—from strategy to human resources to finance, accounting, and operations. They draw on the interdisciplinary research of the Michigan faculty. Yet each book is written so a serious manager can read it quickly and act immediately. I think you will find that they are books that will make a significant difference to you and your organization.

Robert E. Quinn, Consulting Editor
M.E. Tracy Distinguished Professor
University of Michigan Business School

Preface

When we began working on this book, we knew from personal experience that attempts at creativity don't always work as planned. Though plenty of people have analyzed and described how to be creative more easily, these prescriptive approaches never seem to look at the connection between creativity as an activity and the particular characteristics of the task at hand. Psychology, music, education, and many other academic disciplines have made major contributions to the study of creativity, but the kind of creativity these disciplines usually consider is biased toward the fine arts or radical new ideas. The study of creativity in business is somewhat unique in that its singular purpose is to produce superior performance for customers and investors.

We brought together complementary experiences and skills to look more deeply into the dynamics of creativity in organizational settings. Jeff's interest in creativity began twenty-five years ago when he was a student of Rudolf Arnheim, the father of visual thinking. Arnheim suggested that creativity resulted from learning to see in a holistic way. Jeff has continued to study creativity as a manager, consultant, and teacher working with hundreds of leaders who have shared their insights and methods. For a dozen years he has offered courses on creativity at the University of Michigan Business School. Katherine brought her hands-on experience of creativity in the arts and education, working on projects ranging from documentary filmmaking to graphic design to educational software development. Our shared goal was to formulate a theory of creativity practice: an integrated mind-set with accompanying strategies and methods for using creativity to produce valuable results.

We wrote this book for managers who want to develop their people and practices to be more creative at work. What we have seen again and again are businesses desperately trying to make their products, services, and processes more valuable by making them better or new. Although leaders acknowledge and invest in creativity, we seldom see creativity hold a credible place in the business development process. We suggest that this is primarily because creativity often fails to create value. Today's leaders demand that their people produce value, and we believe that creativity can be the path to this end.

This book is unorthodox in three ways: First, the tone of the book is not particularly playful or kitsch. This is because this is not a book about how you can be more like an artist or how you can find your inner child. It is about how you can use creative practices to help yourself and your colleagues produce more valuable results. Second, we suggest that creativity appears in many different forms and produces many different forms of value. Innovation is only one of the valuable outcomes—albeit an important one—produced by creativity. Particularly in business, the manifestations of creativity vary quite a bit, and creativity is most successful when organizational practices are tailored to the specific situation. Third, we propose that creativity occurs at many stages in the process of generating, developing, making, and selling new products, services, and processes, not just in the creation of new ideas. Our point is that if you can't transform a great idea into something tangible, there is little chance that the idea will prove valuable. Isn't this the goal of your business?

Jeff's fieldwork developing creativity practices in firms has taken him to most regions of the world, often where the formulas for creativity that charm American business publications are conspicuously absent. Many new product developers—from Japanese automobile engineers to Finnish cell phone designers— continue to produce industry-leading inventions using practices that Americans would consider to be the antithesis of creativity. These direct encounters with creativity in action have led us to reconsider our cultural biases about creativity and to develop a more multidimensional view. We have discovered that approaching creativity with a comprehensive view requires more work than following a grocery list of best practices, but the payouts are far more substantial.

This book puts creativity within reach of anyone who wants to produce business value. It applies creativity to environments where strategies, performance goals, and processes don't seem to encourage creativity. Most important, it offers a shared language and mind-set to introduce the right approaches for creativity at *your* work.

■ Acknowledgments

We would like to give special thanks to Robert Quinn, who offered us the opportunity to write this book together and whose research is the foundation for this book. The University of Michigan Business School, where we work, provided ongoing resources for our research and writing.

Along the way, many people have jumped in to provide help. We would like to thank, in order of appearance: David Farmer, who gave us moral support, ideas, and organization in the early stages; Sue Reck, Ollie Thomas, and Riza Trinidad, who helped keep us connected; Kim Hannon Parrott, who provided her gifted writing support and a fresh outside perspective; Jim Channon, James Goebel, Rich Sheridan, and James Miller, who loaned their time and expertise; and our helpful reviewers, Robin Glickstein, Mark Jones, Suzanne Merritt, and Michael Thompson. Special mention should go to Darryl Weber, who patiently read the entire book, some parts more than once. His helpful insights and astute feedback strengthened our weakest spots.

The staff at Jossey-Bass Publishers have been remarkable in their support of this series. Their terrific crew includes Cedric Crocker, Kathe Sweeney, Byron Schneider, and Tamara Kastl, ably supported by Pauline Farmer-Koppenol at the University of Michigan Business School. They were especially wise in providing the support of our developmental editor, John Bergez. Everyone should have an editor like John, who is eloquent, insightful, and tireless.

Finally, we thank both our families for their ongoing support. Jeff gives special thanks to Staney for all the hours she spent listening to ideas, asking great questions, and supporting Jeff in his efforts. Katherine thanks her parents, who have supported and encouraged every one of her creative endeavors, from her earliest finger paintings through her first "publishing" ventures and filmmaking escapades to her present pursuits.

May 2002   Jeff DeGraff
Ann Arbor, Michigan   Katherine A. Lawrence

Creativity at Work

The Creativity Map

Discovering *Your* Best Practices
for Creativity at Work

I t has become a truism that organizations today are facing a wider array of competitive pressures than ever before. Businesses believe they cannot afford to do what they have always done. They must be constantly changing and innovating, reinventing themselves at Internet speed to stay ahead of technological change, new competitors from around the globe, and the continually shifting demands of customers and potential employees.

Although no one can deny the accelerated pace of change, in one sense the challenges we face today are nothing new. Organizations have always faced multiple and disjointed—sometimes even opposing—pressures to create value for their customers and stockholders. For centuries, businesses have felt the need to create new products that would succeed in the marketplace. Today's high-tech start-ups and biotech firms are the equivalent of yesterday's automobile inventors or Hollywood pioneers. In every age, the fundamental equation is that creativity creates progress, and progress creates value.

The historical constant is this: what allows a company to respond proactively to diverse pressures is *the development of creativity as a core competence.* By core competence, we mean a well-developed ability or characteristic that is central to your firm's ability to succeed. The focus of creativity may be innovation in the traditional sense—the invention of outstanding products and services—but it may also be the development of new processes, new ways of communicating with customers, or new ways of attracting and retaining the best talent. *Creativity, in short, is the core of all the competencies of your organization because creativity is what makes something better or new.* Creativity is your best path to creating value.

People do a lot of things to try to be creative and to create value. For example, your organization may have trained its employees in creative thinking, or implemented a portfolio system for monitoring projects, or introduced a rapid prototyping system to improve the product development process. These practices may have been helpful on some level, but you may still feel that these efforts have left your company in even more of a muddle. And did they really help you create value? Oftentimes, well-intentioned initiatives lead to unsatisfactory outcomes:

- Creativity programs that leave people feeling good but don't produce tangible results
- Good ideas that can't be commercialized
- Extensive development systems that don't produce breakthrough products or services
- New ventures that don't make sense as a business

- "Flavor of the month" initiatives for quality, change, or culture
- Enterprises that are misaligned with strategy and goals

This book helps you sort through the excess of creativity "solutions" from which your company might select. There are hundreds of approaches to and books on creativity and innovation, many of them based on credible research. Yet most of the published advice on creativity has a key shortcoming: in presenting a set of "best practices," it implies that there is one tried-and-true route to innovation or some other outcome of value. Unfortunately, when companies and managers try to adopt these one-size-fits-all approaches, they usually produce disappointing results. *The truth of creativity is that you must handle each new endeavor differently, selecting an approach to creativity that appropriately matches the situation.* As you will see, different situations are defined in large part by the outcomes you need to produce. The "best practices" and competencies that you use will be different depending on what it is you need to achieve.

This book provides a comprehensive framework—what we will call a map—of creativity at work that will help you recognize your creative situation and act accordingly. With this systematic approach, you can diagnose and assess what competencies and practices will work best for your circumstances. You can identify where you are and navigate toward where you would like to be. Rather than offer a one-size-fits-all list of best practices that may or may not work in your particular situation, we will provide examples from a variety of firms that have used different practices to be creative in different situations. In addition, we will provide tools that you can use to develop the kind of creativity that your own situation requires. Whether you are a top executive who wants to ignite creativity in your firm or a manager wrestling with appropriate creativity practices for your group, this book is for you.

■ **A Working Definition of Creativity**

Think for a moment about what creativity means to you. Do you think about painting, daydreaming, or tinkering in the garage? Who are your role models? Someone like Leonardo da Vinci, Madame Curie, the Dalai Lama, Albert Einstein, or Ella Fitzgerald? What business leaders do you associate with creativity? Perhaps Steve Jobs, Richard Branson, Anita Roddick, or Ben and Jerry? Your answer to these questions implies one or more images of what creativity is.

Many popular images of creativity are biased or incomplete. In business, for example, many people associate creativity exclusively with innovation, in the sense of the introduction of new or dramatically improved products or services. Yet this type of innovation is only one possible result of creativity. Others use the term "innovation" as a blanket description for any creative result. For example, they might say, "The company has accomplished innovations in manufacturing," where the specific outcome might be quality or optimization. This usage, while perhaps imprecise, recognizes a valuable truth that is central to this book: a company, department, or individual can apply creativity toward producing any number of valued outcomes. In fact, depending on your circumstances, other outcomes of creativity may be more valuable than radically new products and services. Just as a flame can warm your home, cook your meat safely, power your car engine, or softly light a room by candlelight, creativity can produce very different things, and innovation in the narrow sense of the word is just one of them.

In this book, we define creativity as *a purposeful activity (or set of activities) that produces valuable products, services, processes, or ideas that are better or new.* The act of creativity can be performed by an individual, a group, or an organization—or all of these working together—to produce a creative outcome, whether innovation, profits, quality, knowledge, or some other desired result.

Whether or not you call the results of creativity "innovations," distinguishing creativity as an activity from the valued outcomes it produces is important for two reasons. First, the distinction allows you to recognize and value opportunities for creativity in many spheres of activity throughout the organization and not just in the development of new or improved products and services. Blurring the distinction between creative activities and their outcomes tends to bias images of creativity toward the domains of art, design, and invention. In fact, creativity is essential in every area of business, from finance to engineering, from product development to order fulfillment and customer service.

Second, dissociating creativity from any one type of outcome allows you to recognize that creativity comes in different forms that produce different valuable results. There is a kind of creativity that is best suited for producing growth, a kind that is best suited for creating speed, and so on. This understanding is key to selecting the creativity practices that will produce the outcomes you desire.

In this book, we call the desired outcomes or goals of creativity *purposes*. Thus we can restate the essential challenge in managing creativity as *matching your creativity practices to your purposes*. Of course, there is a third critical variable: people. Once you know where you need to go (your purposes) and the appropriate means for getting there (the practices), you also need to select or develop people to carry out your initiatives.

Managing creativity, then, is fundamentally about achieving the right mix of purposes, practices, and people. How to achieve that mix is the subject of this book.

■ Mapping Creativity: The Four Profiles

As we have noted, different forms of creativity are appropriate for different purposes. To be specific, our research identifies four main types of creativity, which we have conceptualized as creativity profiles. By *profile*, we mean a description of the biases and preferred creative activities of particular individuals, groups, and organizations, together with the desired creative outcomes of their activities. Figure 1.1 shows a basic map of the four creativity profiles, which we call Imagine, Invest, Improve, and Incubate. We will fill in this map in different ways as we go through the book. Among other things, the map can be used to characterize different kinds of creativity practices and purposes, the values prized within each approach to creativity, and the type of creativity that generally characterizes different organizations, business departments, and even whole industries.

The four profiles also describe the creative tendencies of individuals and groups. That is, you can use the map to locate and describe the creative preferences of individuals, work groups, and whole organizations—both as they are today and as you might like them to be. Moreover, as you will see in Chapter Two, the arrangement of the four profiles on the map is quite deliberate and based on an overall structure.[1] The placement of the profiles on the map helps to clarify the relationships and tensions among the different types of creativity and creative preferences. As we embellish this basic map throughout the book, you will see that it provides you with a powerful management tool.

Let's take a closer look at the four profiles and how they are exemplified by some real companies and individuals. As you read these descriptions, think about your own personal preferences as well as the challenges faced by your organization or work group. Which of the profiles fits you best? Are there some profiles that seem less "creative"? Which profile or profiles best

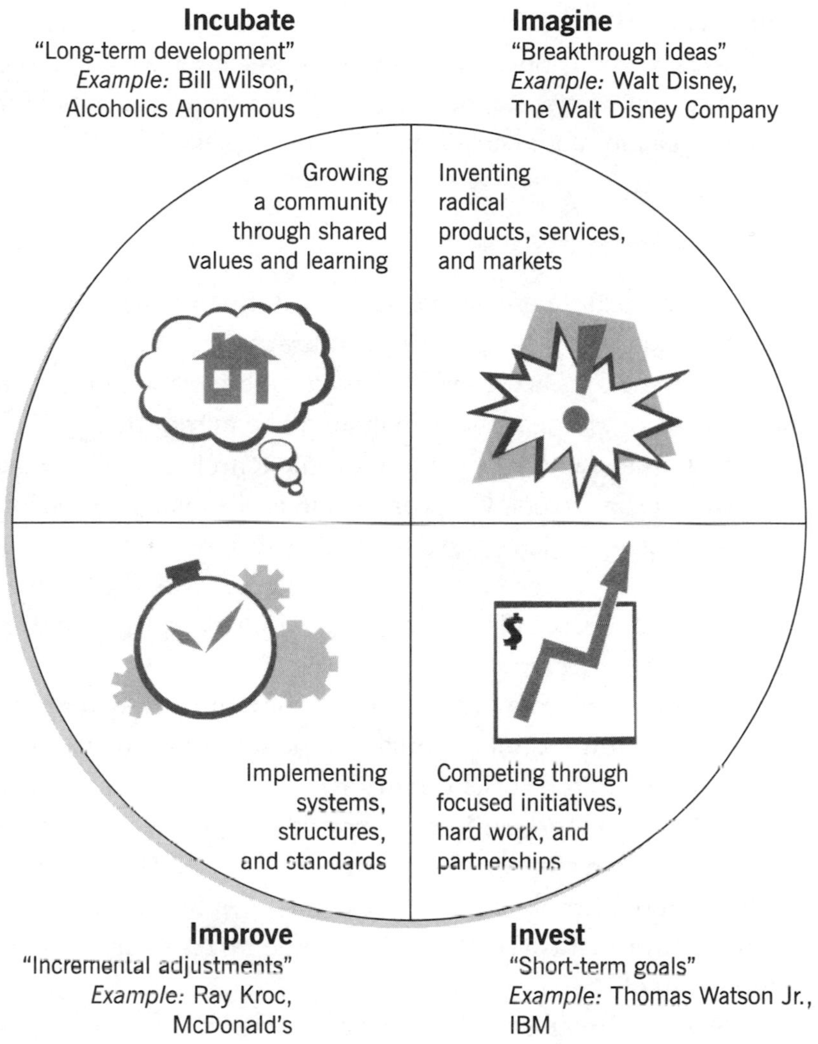

Incubate
"Long-term development"
Example: Bill Wilson,
Alcoholics Anonymous

Imagine
"Breakthrough ideas"
Example: Walt Disney,
The Walt Disney Company

Growing
a community
through shared
values and learning

Inventing
radical
products, services,
and markets

Implementing
systems,
structures,
and standards

Competing through
focused initiatives,
hard work, and
partnerships

Improve
"Incremental adjustments"
Example: Ray Kroc,
McDonald's

Invest
"Short-term goals"
Example: Thomas Watson Jr.,
IBM

Figure 1.1. The Creativity Map

capture your future direction or reflect where your organization most needs to go? Though you may see yourself reflected in more than one profile, first recognizing their differences is essential for making decisions about creativity in your organization.

The Imagine Profile

The Imagine profile encompasses the kinds of purposes and practices that many people think of first when they hear the word *creativity.* This is the profile of radical breaks with the past and breakthrough ideas that can change the marketplace.

Individuals with the Imagine profile tend to be generalists or artistic types who enjoy exploring and easily change direction when solving a problem. The culture that supports their work is characterized by experimentation and speculation; the focus is on generating ideas. This group is often in R&D units or entrepreneurial activities.

Imagine companies seek to create something new that has been thought impossible. Typical purposes are innovation or growth. They strive to orient their products, services, and ideas to the future. Leaders build the organization by developing a compelling vision and emphasizing new ideas and technologies, flexibility, and adaptability. Imagine companies capitalize on turbulent environments. The Imagine profile taken to an extreme becomes chaotic.

Disney's Grand Experiment.[2] Walt Disney saw the future first. The man who drew Mickey Mouse also created the first full-length animated film, the theme park, and the modern multimedia company. His name has become synonymous with leading-edge ventures, from *Snow White and the Seven Dwarfs* to the Epcot Center. Disney created such optimistic, intimate experiences inside a futuristic utopia that children and adults eagerly await each Disney product.

Disney's gift was his ability to recognize a good opportunity on the horizon. Confident in his vision, he took on enormous risk to undertake his ventures. In contrast to his public persona, Disney was a complex and controlling leader whose vision carried him from childhood poverty to commercial artist to entrepreneur to media mogul. Disney was one of the first to try new entertainment technologies: quality sound, Technicolor, advanced animation techniques, and robotics. The result has been an organization that could embrace a trend before it happened, growing from film to television to amusement parks.

Perhaps his greatest triumph was his last. Disney World and the Epcot Center were considered modern miracles of "imagineering" and urban planning when they were built. Disney converted the skeptics and enlisted them in his mission. In the process, he turned the mosquito-infested swamps of central Florida into one of the top tourist destinations in the world. Today, his characters and emblems are some of the most readily recognized brands.

The Invest Profile

The Invest profile encompasses the kinds of people and practices that many people associate with Wall Street. This is a profile that shows the intensity of competition and achievement—everyone is either a winner or a loser.

Individuals with the Invest profile are focused on performance and goals. Their culture emphasizes these results and the discipline necessary to create them. This group typically includes members of the finance department and marketing. People with the Invest profile are competitive and love a good challenge, which motivates them toward a speedy and profitable outcome.

Invest companies seek to create quickly before competitors can. Typical purposes focus on profits through market share, revenues, and brand equity, or through speed of response. Leaders build the organization by clarifying objectives and improving the firm's competitive position through hard work and productivity. These companies seek to deliver results to stake-holders as quickly as possible. Beating the competition is not only a matter of strategy but also a matter of pride. The Invest profile taken to an extreme becomes a sweatshop.

Watson's Challenge.[3] In the early years of computing, Thomas Watson Jr.'s IBM ruled the technology universe through aggressive strategy and relentless marketing. The troops at "Big Blue" moved faster than anyone else. Leading through ambition and challenge, Watson was a master of competition. At Watson's IBM, if you weren't first, you weren't much. He promoted "winners" and expected them to perform by meeting each new backbreaking deadline. His famous corporate mantra "Think" was more than just something to aspire to; it was an admonition to anyone who did not develop the world-class competencies to leap over all obstacles.

Watson's father had founded IBM, and during the Depression years, he built it into a cornerstone of the American white-collar workplace by producing superior business machines such as tabulators. Thomas Jr. was anything but ambitious in his youth, moving from school to school before graduating from Brown University. After a brief stint as a sales manager at IBM, he enlisted in the armed services, serving as a pilot. There he developed his celebrated courage while flying missions throughout the Pacific. He became an aide to the Air Force's Inspector General, where he introduced flight simulators to aeronautical training and developed his sharp planning skills. He returned to IBM a motivated leader who would never again retreat.

IBM did not invent the computer; others started that revolution. But under Watson, IBM set the pace for technological advancement and learned to keep an enormous enterprise changing constantly. Watson spent three times IBM's annual revenues to create a new line of computers; effectively changing the industry. He brought projects in on time, and even ousted his younger brother Dick as head of engineering and manufacturing when a key project was off schedule.

Competence and motivation led to performance at Watson's IBM in the 1950s and 1960s, and performance typically led to success and promotion. By the time Watson stepped down at IBM, it had destroyed its core business in favor of a new one, and set the quick pace for all technology companies that would follow in its footsteps.

The Improve Profile

The Improve profile represents incremental creativity—taking something that exists and modifying it to make it better. This is the profile of large, complex organizations that create products and services that must not fail.

People in the Improve profile are systematic, careful, and practical. Their culture focuses on planning, creating systems and processes, and enforcing compliance. Improve people are typically found in engineering departments or in operational groups that must maintain complex systems and reduce errors. They seek to keep things running and efficient.

Improve companies seek to create something better so as to build on the present. Typical purposes are quality or optimization, sometimes expressed as predictability or productivity. Leaders build the organization by optimizing processes, cutting costs, and establishing rules and procedures. Role definition is important here. These companies tend to elaborate or extend existing products with minor variations. The Improve profile taken to an extreme becomes an immobile bureaucracy.

Kroc's Hamburger System.[4] No matter where you may be in the world, two things are certain: one, there is a McDonald's hamburger restaurant around the corner; and two, the burgers taste exactly the same as they do every other place you've eaten one. Ray Kroc, who grew the McDonald's restaurant chain, helped transform American dining from a personalized sit-down experience into standardized fast food for a generation on the go. Instead of having chefs prepare food as an art, Kroc turned cooking on its head and made food service an engineering science.

A former piano player, ambulance driver, and paper-cup salesman, Kroc obtained exclusive marketing rights for a high-speed multimixer machine and sold it across America for seventeen years. In 1954 in San Bernardino, California, he sold eight mixers to a remarkable restaurant owned by two brothers, Dick and Mac McDonald. The restaurant, McDonald's, had a limited menu, focusing on a few items: burgers, french fries, soft drinks, and milk shakes. Kroc saw a system that could easily be replicated. After buying out the McDonald brothers in 1961 for $2.7 million, Kroc set to the task of refining the system. Kroc laid out the goof-proof McDonald's Way, including restaurant design, marketing, procurement, and training at Hamburger University, a requirement for all franchisees before running a restaurant. One size fit all.

The first McDonald's had no tables or silverware. There were drive-up stands where you could get a decent meal for less than a dollar. Dine-in and drive-through options were added later, but quality and service remained the cornerstones of Kroc's company. Clean restrooms made the formula complete. Kroc's process of getting it done right made McDonald's the largest food service company in the world.

Kroc didn't invent fast food—White Castle, Howard Johnson's, and other chains had been around long before McDonald's. Kroc had an ability to understand the complexities of the system, both in terms of food preparation and restaurant development. He could improve processes at every turn so that a person could learn the science of making food quickly, with few errors. The result of his process improvement and systems is a consistent product and experience. Like Henry Ford, who used the assembly line to transform automobile manufacturing, Kroc achieved peak performance through his understanding of process.

The Incubate Profile

The Incubate profile encompasses the kinds of people who believe in something greater than the business itself and run their business to reflect those values. This is the profile associated with having a great place to work and learn.

People in the Incubate profile are committed to their community, focusing on shared values and communication. Their culture strives to learn over time, and once these competencies are established, the amount of time required to understand a situation and act appropriately is shortened. They are likely to feel that creativity should be timeless. This group is often in human resources, training, or organizational development functions.

Incubate companies seek to create something sound that is appreciated by the community. Typical purposes are community and knowledge, achieved by drawing on communication, cooperation, and learning-oriented partnerships. Leaders build the organization by encouraging trust, commitment, and relationships, and by nurturing a community of empowered individuals. Their unified behavior produces a strong organizational image in the marketplace. Customers may be considered partners in an extended community. The Incubate profile taken to an extreme becomes a pleasure cruise that goes nowhere.

Bill W.'s Community.[5] Bill Wilson may have saved more lives around the world than the leader of any state or enterprise in the twentieth century. Known as "Bill W." to members of Alcoholics Anonymous, the organization he co-founded with Dr. Robert Smith, Bill Wilson proved to be a healer on an incredible social and cultural scale. What made Wilson so extraordinary is not that he learned how to stop his own raging alcoholism but that he formed an organization with the sole purpose of teaching others how to overcome their addictions and supporting them in their efforts. In the process, he overcame his own drinking problem. Today, twelve-step programs are applied to all kinds of fixations including gambling, eating disorders, drug abuse, and sex addictions.

Wilson had come from a family with a history of alcoholism. When he was a boy, his father and mother abandoned him and left him with his grandparents. First as a soldier, then as a businessman, Wilson drank to ease his depression and to celebrate his success. This dependence on alcohol soon made him unemployable, and he turned to panhandling and living off relatives. One day in 1934, while staying at a hospital in Manhattan, Wilson had a spiritual awakening that led to the development of the twelve-step remedy for alcoholism. After years of intoxication, Wilson had been "dry" for five months when he went to Akron, Ohio, on business. The deal he was pursuing fell through, and he wanted to have a drink. In his panic, Wilson had a revelation that he could save himself only by helping another alcoholic, because that person would understand his suffering. He tracked down Dr. Robert Smith, both a physician and an alcoholic, and together they endured without a drink.

Soon Wilson and Smith were meeting with other alcoholics in Akron, and they began to codify and share the principles that lead to sobriety. After years of revision, a book called *Alcoholics Anonymous* was successfully published, and the organization from which it took its name received limited support from John D. Rockefeller and national attention from magazine articles in the popular press. To the end, Wilson took no money for his coaching or good counsel.

Today Alcoholics Anonymous has more than two million members in 150 countries. Meetings are held wherever informal space can be found: churches, schools, gyms, and houses. Members still identify themselves by their first names and share stories about the most intimate details of their lives. Wilson, too, preferred to remain anonymous and always referred to himself as a student, never a teacher. Wilson showed his vulnerabilities and shared his pain with others so that they could also bring their demons out of the shadows. Bill Wilson's leadership style was to welcome involvement and openness, encouraging a culture that invested in education through common experience, leading to increased knowledge and healing.

■ Recognizing and Valuing Different Kinds of Creativity

As these four stories illustrate, not all creativity is the "breakthrough" type associated with the Imagine profile. Other kinds of creativity are equally valid and equally important, depending on the circumstances. Walt Disney may have reflected the "Imagine" profile, but his company's success results in part from the fact that this was the type of creativity that suited his business challenge. By the same token, Ray Kroc didn't need breakthrough creativity so much as he needed the kind of creativity that takes an existing idea, improves on it, and results in a superbly efficient and dependable system. Indeed, Kroc might have failed in the fast-food business had he brought to it a Disney style of creativity.

The point is that the creative practices and competencies you use will determine the outcomes you get. If you have specific purposes in mind, you have to use the right practices, and to achieve the right practices, you need the right people. It's like losing weight. Each year in the United States, thousands of people set a resolution to lose weight, yet they don't achieve it. They focus on the goal, but not on developing the ability to achieve it. If, instead, they ate healthy foods and exercised at the gym, most of them would lose weight whether they wanted to or not. In fact, the irony is that anyone who only employs a set of practices will achieve the outcomes specific to those practices, even if the purposes were never defined.

Being able to identify and value different kinds of creativity is a first step toward better creativity management. Once you recognize the basic forms of creativity, you can begin to think much more clearly about how to make appropriate creativity happen in your firm or your work group. At any given time, you can diagnose the type of creativity you need, the right people for the job, and the specific practices to try. The next section elaborates on this idea.

■ Putting the Creativity Profiles to Work

The practical importance of our creativity map can be summed up in one word: direction. The map should help you to get your people and practices to work toward the same purposes.

First, each of the creativity profiles is particularly well suited for certain organizational *purposes*, or valued outcomes. Your business purposes—the outcomes you want to achieve— should drive the type of creativity you need. Too often, business purposes fail to drive creativity initiatives. Instead of focusing on what they must achieve, people limit themselves to their established notions of creativity, using the approach that has worked for them in the past or that is based on how they are most effective. But the value of an approach depends on what it is supposed to accomplish. In terms of the map, the Imagine profile is suitable when you focus on innovation and growth. But when your primary need is to create profits or produce a fast response, then you should look to the Invest profile. When you seek optimization and quality, you should look to the Improve profile. And when your goal is to cultivate a community or build knowledge, you should look to the Incubate profile. Being clear about your purposes is a big step toward capitalizing on your creative resources.

Second, different kinds of creativity *practices* are appropriate for different profiles. You may have heard of, or even used, creativity practices like jump-starting or portfolios, but using such practices intelligently requires understanding what kinds of purposes they are best able to fulfill. Once you locate where you are and where you need to be on the creativity map, you can choose the specific creativity practices that are appropriate for your situation.

Third, creativity is about *people.* Any creativity initiative depends on the talents, strengths, and inclinations of the people involved. Most of us tend to have a bias in one direction or another. This is not to say that we can't grow into other types of creativity, but as a leader or manager you need a way of identifying people's existing strengths and inclinations, determining the mix you need for any given purpose, and, where appropriate, helping people develop strengths in new types of creativity. The creativity map gives you and your colleagues a shared sense of the "geography" of creativity and a shared language for talking about it.

Ultimately, of course, your task as a leader or a manager is not only to identify a single type of creativity that you need to cultivate at any given moment, but to find the most effective blend of the different creative competencies and practices that you need to fulfill all your purposes. As a manager, you are concerned with identifying and developing the types of creativity that are right for your departmental and organizational circumstances. Undoubtedly you will see a role for your own creativity and the creativity of those who work with you. At the same time, you will want to implement broader practices that support the overall achievement of your purposes. You may require methods that are different from past solutions. Thus multiple creative practices may form the basis for achieving your organization's purposes.

Table 1.1 summarizes these three key variables and provides an overview of the way we will explore them in this book. Chapter Two explains how to assess your creativity situation—that is, your needs and your existing resources. Chapters Three through Six each develop one of the creativity profiles. For each profile, we present detailed accounts of two exemplary practices and illustrate them through the real-life examples that are listed in the table. Your task, going forward, is to understand when to apply different approaches. The right approach, at the right time, will produce the results that you desire. We return to this point in Chapter Seven, which offers guidance for how to manage and integrate different types of people and practices within an organization so as to have creativity that works.

In summary, how to apply and succeed with creativity is not easily solved by a one-size-fits-all list of best practices. The purpose of your creativity and the practices that you implement are likely to be different depending on your situation. The creativity map will help you match your approach to your situation, while the practices we describe will provide both inspiration and specific tools for maximizing creativity. As with any map, it may take you a while as you get your bearings, but once you know the lay of the land, you can go anywhere. You can choose how to navigate toward success.

CHAPTER SUMMARY

Creativity has always been an essential way for organizations to make progress and, in turn, create value for stakeholders inside and outside the organization. Creativity as a core competence can help a company create products, services, processes, or ideas that are better or new.

Creativity means different things to different people. We define creativity as a purposeful activity (or set of activities) that produces valuable products, services, processes, or ideas that are better or new. Distinguishing

Table 1.1. Summary of the Four Creativity Profiles

	Purposes	Practices	People	Organizational Examples
Imagine (Chapter Three)	• Innovation • Growth	• Jump-starting • Forecasting	• Generalists • Enjoy exploring • Willing to change direction • Like diversity	• Fluke • Reuters
Invest (Chapter Four)	• Speed • Profits	• Partnering • Portfolios	• Performance-oriented • Mindful of goals • Disciplined • Like challenges	• eBay • idealab!
Improve (Chapter Five)	• Quality • Optimization	• Modular design and development • Process improvement systems	• Systematic • Technical • Practical • Like processes	• Interface Systems • Toyota
Incubate (Chapter Six)	• Community • Knowledge	• Talent scouting • Idea spaces	• Share values • Community-oriented • Communicative • Like learning	• Home Depot • Hallmark

□

creativity as an activity from its specific outcomes, such as innovative products and services, demonstrates how creativity happens in every area of business and produces many valuable outcomes. Our research has identified four basic types of creativity, which we characterize as profiles: Imagine, Invest, Improve, and Incubate. Each of these profiles is best suited to certain kinds of business purposes, and each has its own distinctive practices. Furthermore, the four profiles can help you understand the creative preferences of organizations, departments, work groups, and individuals.

As you proceed through this book, you will see how the creativity map can help you assess where you are, understand where you need to go, and navigate toward your desired outcomes. The specific practices we present will provide some of the vehicles that can get you there.

A fundamental tenet of our approach to creativity is that the "best practices" for creativity are the ones that match the demands of your particular situation. To achieve specific purposes, you have to use the right practices, and to achieve the right practices, you need the right people. The next chapter explains how to diagnose your situation and assess where you are with respect to creativity.

Assessing Your Creativity Situation

Mapping Where You Are and Where You Need to Go

S o far, you should have a general sense of the four creativity profiles, but to put the creativity map into action, you'll need to assess your own creativity situation. This chapter will provide a more detailed picture of the profiles and the dimensions that shape the purposes, practices, and people in each. Also, it will provide an assessment that you can use to better understand your own creativity and the creativity of the people you manage.

■ Defining Your Purposes

The different purposes of creativity correspond with the four profiles. For example, four different people considering the potential of the Human Genome Project might see different opportunities:

- To change the future of human life through breakthrough genetic interventions (Imagine)
- To sell new drugs (Invest)
- To reduce the side effects of medical treatments (Improve)
- To foster a community of scientists committed to ethical applications of this discovery (Incubate)

Some of these purposes do not, at first glance, seem "creative." Instead, try thinking of these purposes as different lenses or filters that color one's worldview. That is, what is valuable about creativity is different depending on your perspective. See Exhibit 2.1 for a description of each of the most common purposes corresponding to each of the four creativity profiles.

Because purposes are deeply connected to particular perspectives or biases, at any one time organizations usually have to manage a tapestry of shifting tensions. For example, the director of marketing may focus on the purpose of growth, while the director of manufacturing may be preoccupied with optimization. Over time, an organization's overall purposes may shift, too. These differences across functions and time can generate misunderstandings about the organization's priorities, even though the purposes may not be explicitly stated.

In particular, purposes at opposite corners of Exhibit 2.1 tend to have opposing means for achieving them, and using creativity to create value in one area may actually destroy value in another. For example, when a firm is determined to achieve speedy solutions (Invest), it is likely to sacrifice the opportunity to develop deep knowledge (Incubate). Similarly, highly specu-

Exhibit 2.1. Purposes Defined: Each Profile's Valuable Outcomes

These purposes are what each profile considers to be the reason why they do what they do and what they hope to achieve.

Incubate	Imagine
Community: Establishing and maintaining shared values and culture. Common ways of achieving this are networking, empowerment, and team building.	*Innovation:* Making novel products and services. Common ways of achieving this are creative problem solving, new product development, and change management.
Knowledge: Developing understanding and skills. Common ways of achieving this are training, organizational learning, and mentoring.	*Growth:* Prospecting for new and future market opportunities. Common ways of achieving this are strategic forecasting, trend analysis, and initiating organizational change.
Quality: Eliminating errors. Common ways of achieving this are process controls, systems, and technology. *Optimization:* Using resources in the best way possible. Common ways of achieving this are procedures, budgeting, and organizational design.	*Speed:* Moving quickly to capture an opportunity. Common ways of achieving this are mergers and acquisitions, product management, and giving the customers what they want. *Profits:* Maximizing shareholder earnings. Common ways of achieving this are using goals and metrics, strategic resource allocation, and portfolio management.
Improve	Invest

lative ideas for innovations (Imagine) make it difficult to achieve optimization or quality (Improve). Such opposing goals may produce conflict about the right practices to use because pursuing any particular purpose entails trade-offs.

However, it is common for a firm to pursue all four kinds of purposes in different degrees at any given time. For example, a firm with R&D, representing the goals of innovation and growth, usually has a production department too, which represents quality and optimization. We can illustrate this same dynamic over a period of time by following the life cycle of a start-up firm. At first, the firm would pursue Imagine purposes of innovation and growth because it lacks the range of products or services and the production scale to compete with existing companies. Over time, the company will focus increasingly on Invest purposes such as pursuing sound financial business strategies and Incubate purposes such as cultivating a good workforce. Eventually, when the firm has grown sufficiently, it must develop systems because it has to handle complex issues such as managing large volumes of production, typical Improve purposes.

Unfortunately, some firms do not have a big enough picture of what their purpose could be. The development of the Xerox Alto is an example of narrowing the big picture too much and failing to redefine purposes.[1] In the 1970s, Xerox developed the first "modern" personal computer at its Palo Alto Research Center. Dubbed the Alto, the computer had a mouse, an Ethernet connection, a graphical user interface with a bit-mapped display, and local file storage. However, Xerox didn't see personal computing as relevant to its core business of copiers. It was engaged in fierce competition to patent newer copier-related technology and directed its resources accordingly. Ironically, much of the core market that Xerox had hoped to capture with its improved copiers migrated toward desktop publishing. This shift happened partly because Xerox's competitors exploited the inventions that Xerox had created and failed to commercialize. Xerox had pursued an agenda based on an outdated concept of the value it could offer while the external forces of technology, competitors, and customers were moving toward value in other forms. In the end, Xerox had not failed to invent, it had failed to understand how its invention related to changing forces outside the firm.

In Chapter One, we suggested that purposes—the valued outcomes that you want to achieve—should determine what creativity practices you use.[2] Consequently, you need to decide what the purposes of your organization or work unit should be. This can be both complicated and simple. On one hand, you need to sift through many factors to identify your purposes, but once you identify them, your purposes will seem quite clear.

Your purposes are created by a combination of external and internal forces. Consider the situation of the organization as a whole. Externally, a variety of market, stakeholder, and environmental demands will determine which purposes (desired outcomes) are most valuable given the circumstances. Internally, the organization's characteristics—including its industry, growth, and location—and its values will also shape its purposes. Figure 2.1 summarizes these external and internal forces, while Figure 2.2 shows the situations they produce.

External Forces

Although no one likes to believe it, a firm's power to select its purposes is limited because stronger, more compelling external forces, such as a disruptive technology or market conditions, may determine what is valuable. For example, when the Asian currency crisis hit suddenly in 1997, Coca-Cola could not meet its sales targets in the Asian market. The stock market was unkind to Coca Cola for missing its earning projections. Still, there was little that the firm could do to offset the sales decline. The environmental circumstances were much more powerful than a single corporation could manage. During such dramatic shifts, it is easy to see the environmental forces at work. Smaller day-to-day movements such as stock market fluctuations, changes in demography, or technological evolution are equally powerful but more difficult to perceive or anticipate.

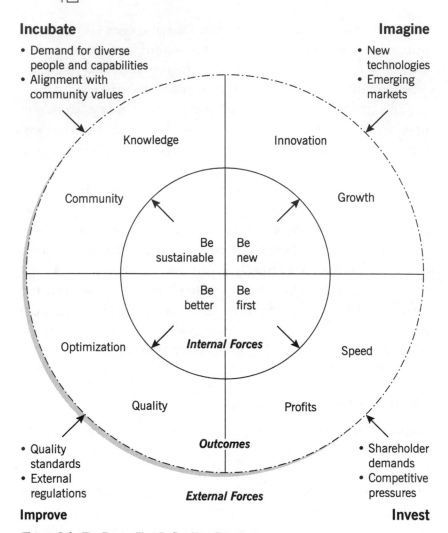

Incubate
- Demand for diverse people and capabilities
- Alignment with community values

Imagine
- New technologies
- Emerging markets

Knowledge

Innovation

Community

Growth

Be sustainable | Be new

Be better | Be first

Internal Forces

Optimization

Speed

Quality

Profits

Outcomes

- Quality standards
- External regulations

External Forces

- Shareholder demands
- Competitive pressures

Improve

Invest

Figure 2.1. The Forces That Define Your Purposes

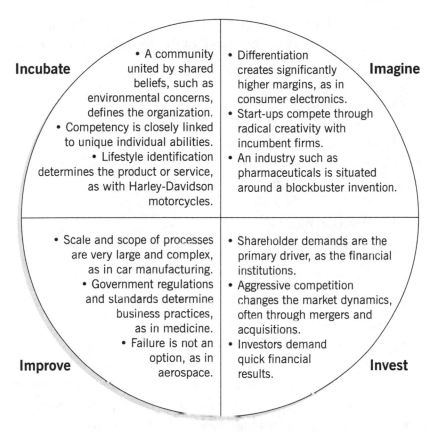

The situations described here are common indicators that practices associated with a particular profile would be appropriate for your situation.

Figure 2.2. Types of Situations Created by Internal and External Forces

When leaders of a firm define their purposes, they look at the external forces that affect the organization. Such forces might include

- Competition
- Technology
- Demographics
- Government regulations
- Consumer demands
- Politics
- Macroeconomics
- Shareholders
- Social concerns

Understanding how external forces like these help shape your firm's purposes is key to appropriately directing and redirecting creativity. Think of it like surfing. Surfing requires a limited amount of equipment and considerable skill, but most important, it requires the ocean to make it work. The surfer doesn't make surfing possible, the surfer working with the ocean does. A surfer has to constantly look to the horizon for waves that are barely perceptible. The surfer adjusts the board to time the wave. Similarly, even though leaders and managers have limited control over forces external to their organization, they still must be mindful of them and adjust their purposes accordingly.

Internal Forces

A company's history produces two types of internal forces that shape that company's purposes: organizational characteristics and organizational values. To some extent, these internal forces also determine which external forces might be most relevant at a given time.

Organizational characteristics. A company is most obviously defined by its competencies—what it is capable of making, selling, and supporting. An organization's purposes will also depend on the nature of what it produces—whether it is conceptual, technical, or something in between. One company's purposes may differ from its competitors' if it is different in terms of size or location—smaller firms may be able to change more readily and regional customs influence what practices are acceptable. Moreover, purposes are defined and redefined over the course of a project by the dominant department at a given time. From a broad perspective, however, certain characteristics of organizations, functions, and even some industries tend to align with one or another creativity profile, as shown in Figure 2.3.

Organizational values. Organizations are also driven by their values—not the value associated with the purposes being sought, but what different organizations emphasize as important to what they do and how they do it. The tug of war between competing values in different departments or at different times is a source of misunderstanding about what constitutes corporate creativity, and the organization must consider these values when defining its purposes. For example, manufacturing managers may seek optimization and quality through reengineering. These people value incremental and systematic approaches to creativity. Conversely, those in marketing may see innovation and growth as the most desirable outcomes and they value the introduction of radically differentiated products to new markets. To them, creativity should be more experimental and emergent. Both groups are driven by their values in addition to the purposes that will achieve value for stakeholders. Figure 2.4 shows some of the values that are typical of each of the four profiles.

■ Defining Your Practices

Managing creativity should seem more straightforward when you can recognize how your purposes are influenced by both internal and external factors. However, the so-called management

Incubate

Examples
- McKinsey & Co.
- The Body Shop
- Patagonia

- Firms with a great reputation as employers
- "Lifestyle" companies (those that stand by their values)
- Firms that offer their employees' intelligence and skills (consulting firms)
- Religious organizations
- Educational institutions

Imagine

Examples
- GlaxoSmithKline
- Nokia
- Pixar

- Start-ups
- Biotechs
- Fashion industry
- Consumer electronics
- New product design
- Advertising firms
- Entertainment

- Large-scale manufacturers
- Commodity-driven industries (oil)
- Infrastructure support services (air traffic control)
- Heavily regulated industries (utilities)
- Engineering-based sectors
- Systems integrators
- Medical centers

- Financial services
- Investment banks
- Publicly traded firms
- Industries with few dominant competitors
- Brand-based competition
- Companies attempting to consolidate via acquisitions or hostile takeovers

Examples
- Boeing
- The Mayo Clinic
- U.S. Army

Improve

Examples
- Microsoft
- Citigroup
- Procter & Gamble

Invest

Inside the circle are characteristics that would help you recognize departments or companies in each profile. The specific examples are companies that are typically identified as having these characteristics.

Figure 2.3. Firms and Industries Characteristic of Each Creativity Profile

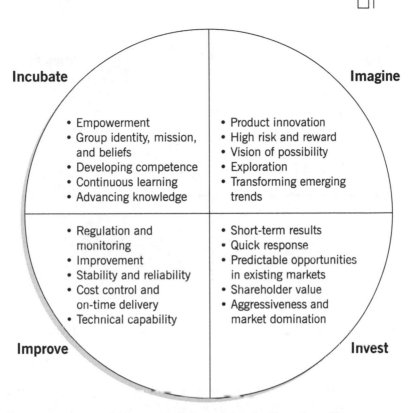

Incubate

- Empowerment
- Group identity, mission, and beliefs
- Developing competence
- Continuous learning
- Advancing knowledge

Imagine

- Product innovation
- High risk and reward
- Vision of possibility
- Exploration
- Transforming emerging trends

Improve

- Regulation and monitoring
- Improvement
- Stability and reliability
- Cost control and on-time delivery
- Technical capability

Invest

- Short-term results
- Quick response
- Predictable opportunities in existing markets
- Shareholder value
- Aggressiveness and market domination

These are valued activities and beliefs associated with each profile.

Figure 2.4. What Is Valued In Each Creativity Profile

science typically advocates the dangerous illusion that you have complete control over your circumstances. It is wiser to acknowledge that you can't control what happens externally and do your best to address these uncertainties with appropriate organizational practices. To select these practices, it is helpful to understand the dynamics that shape the four profiles and why the profiles are defined as they are.

Figure 2.5 reveals the underlying theoretical framework of the creativity map. The figure organizes the four profiles in terms of two main dimensions, *focus* (internal versus external) and *approach* (divergent versus convergent). The combination of

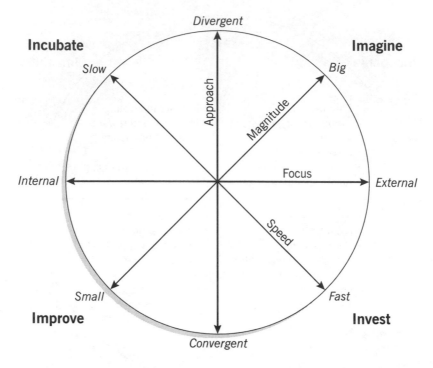

Two main dimensions shape each profile: *focus* (the orientation of organizational practices and people) and *approach* (how goals are accomplished). The combination of these dimensions produce two secondary dimensions: *magnitude* ("How much?") and *speed* ("How fast?"). These dimensions can apply to purposes, practices, and people.

Figure 2.5. **Dimensions of Creativity**

these dimensions creates two additional subdimensions that imply the *magnitude* of the result and the *speed* with which it is achieved. To see what this means, take a look at these dimensions as they are reflected in each profile's practices.

Focus: Internal Versus External

The dimension of *focus* accounts for the orientation of organizational practices. Some practices tend to focus internally, that is, on the organization's own characteristics and capacities. Others tend to focus externally, on the demands of the situation.

Internal focus. The Incubate and Improve (on the left side of the map) profiles have an internal focus. Practices with an internal focus are oriented toward developing underlying competencies—such as systems and culture—that support their purposes. Such practices endorse the idea that creativity operates within the boundaries of the firm's processes and values and enhances their performance over time.

External focus. The Imagine and Invest profiles (on the right side of the map) have an external focus. These practices adapt to forces external to the organization, anticipating and prospecting new opportunities, ideas, and markets. Such practices focus on the emerging competitive situation. An externally focused firm may view creativity as a means to an end: the development of a product, the accumulation of wealth, or overcoming a barrier.

Approach: Divergent Versus Convergent

The dimension of *approach* accounts for how organizational practices accomplish their goals. When a situation is new or unpredictable, the best practice is to search for all possible solutions by taking an approach that diverges from a starting point. When a situation calls for a single solution or a limited response, converging on an optimal solution is the necessary approach.

Divergent approach. The Imagine and Incubate profiles (on the top half of the map) take a divergent approach. Practices with a divergent approach are typically directed toward exploring options. Their methods and goals need to be flexible and allow for emerging ideas and dynamic possibilities. Diversity is valued for its ability to help generate original ideas. People who favor this approach tend to think broadly and imaginatively, cultivating their ability to handle unpredictable situations by drawing on knowledge and insight.

Convergent approach. The Invest and Improve profiles (on the bottom half of the map) take a convergent approach. Practices with a convergent approach are directed toward clearly defined goals and systems. Their methods rely on structure, processes, and technologies to achieve low-risk forms of value. They value consistency and efficiency. People who favor this approach rely on reason, methodical behavior, and goal orientation because they are not just looking for a solution—they are looking for the right solution.

Secondary Dimensions: Magnitude and Speed

Blending the dimensions of focus and approach produces two secondary dimensions: *speed* and *magnitude.* Often, these two dimensions help organizations and individuals figure out what practices suit them best because they distinguish how quickly value creation must occur and what benefits it must achieve. The questions "how much?" and "how fast?" serve as a quick-and-dirty way of identifying the profile that most aptly describes your situation. If your answer to one question is more specific than the other, then that answer points to your likely profile. For example, if your answer was, "It doesn't matter how big of an impact I make, but I need to deliver a product fast," then you fit the Invest profile. Let's look at these two dimensions in a bit more detail.

Magnitude. "Big" or "new" creativity produces diversification and differentiation through breakthrough innovations or dislocating the status quo. "Small" or "better" creativity focuses on enhanced quality, productivity, and efficiency by improving and maintaining existing processes and products. The Imagine profile is distinguished by big, new creativity, and the Improve profile is characterized by small, better creativity.

Speed. "Fast" or "short-term" creativity produces immediate results and predictable shareholder returns using quantifiable measures and rigorous project management. "Slow" or "long-term" creativity produces qualitatively improved abilities, learning, and sustainability through the development and dissemination of strong values and culture. The Invest profile is distinguished by fast, short-term creativity, and the Incubate profile is characterized by slow, long-term creativity.

Summarizing the Dimensions

Together, the dimensions illustrated in Figure 2.5 can give you a deeper understanding of the creativity profiles and the purposes, practices, and people that fit them. The dimensions can help you identify your company's overall purposes and assess whether you have the appropriate competencies (in the form of practices and people) to achieve them. The dimensions of the creativity map can also help you understand creative tensions within the firm. Many companies have product development, finance, manufacturing, and training departments. All these departments might contribute toward delivering the same product, but the way they produce value for the firm is categorically different. To summarize, here are capsule descriptions of each profile.

Imagine purposes—innovation and growth—drive practices to have an external focus and a divergent approach. Crisis, new information, or uncertainty compel organizations in this profile to change, take risks, and experiment. Creativity produces results of large magnitude, at a speed that may vary.

Invest purposes—profits and speed—drive practices to have an external focus and a convergent approach. A stable yet challenging environment pushes organizations in this profile to focus on disciplined financial management and acquiring capabilities, access to markets, and first-mover advantage. Creativity produces fast results of moderate magnitude.

Improve purposes—optimization and quality—drive practices to have an internal focus and a convergent approach. Complex operations or products, government regulations, and high standards make these organizations focus on cost control, standards, processes, and technological tools. Creativity produces results of small, predictable magnitude at a moderate speed.

Incubate purposes—community and knowledge—drive practices to have an internal focus and a divergent approach. A recognition that people and their abilities are at the core of success motivate organizations in this profile to empower their employees and build their capabilities through multiple methods. Creativity produces results at variable speed—slow during development of these practices but faster once relationships are established—and the results tend to be moderate.

Practices are important for achieving your purposes, but behind the scenes, people are what make practices work. You probably work with a variety of people who have different preferences in how they approach creativity, and it's useful to be able to recognize the creativity profiles in action.

■ Defining Personal Profiles

The creativity map can also help you understand individuals' biases with respect to creative activity. As you read the following descriptions of people in each profile, we hope you will recognize people you know at work. Seeing how individuals can support or undermine creativity practices will help you compose a team that will help you achieve your purposes.

Bear in mind that a person's creative profile represents a set of biases and preferred activities, which should not be confused with abilities. A person may be inclined toward a particular creative profile but may lack the skill or experience necessary for effective creativity within that profile. Furthermore, individuals differ in the flexibility with which they can move from one profile to another. As you read, think about how your workplace relies on one or more profiles. Do you have the opportunity to work in your preferred ways? Do you have coworkers who take on some roles while you assume others? How do you work with people who are in profiles that are opposite your favored one? Also consider the match between individuals, their job duties, and the type of creativity needed for your purposes. Top performers at your workplace may be in an area that fits their strongest preferences, while low performers may be working on tasks that don't suit their preferences very well. Considering these questions will help you apply these profiles to the way that you manage your own work and your collaborations.

People in the Imagine Profile

People with Imagine preferences (Figure 2.6) want to create breakthrough results. They are catalysts for change and for creating new products, services, and markets. Often they move fast, but sometimes they do not. Associated with the entrepreneurs of start-up, high-tech, and biotech companies, people with Imagine preferences are energized by turbulent and fast-changing conditions. When the future is unclear, their flexibility, ingenuity, and imagination helps them achieve a successful strategy. They judge their success on the inventiveness and future-readiness of their products, services, and ideas.

People in the Invest Profile

People with Invest preferences (Figure 2.7) move fast to create moderate results. They are tough competitors who quickly produce superior financial results. People with Invest preferences are often found in publicly traded companies that must demonstrate short-term profitability for shareholders. They perceive the external world as hostile and customers as self-interested and choosy. They operate primarily through disciplined

Positive Characteristics and Types
- Clever
- Optimistic
- Enthusiastic
- Quick
- Expressive
- Opinionated
- Passionate
- Visionary
- Dreamers
- Big-picture thinkers
- Planners
- Generalists

Negative Characteristics and Types
- Reckless
- Superficial
- Unrealistic
- Uncommitted
- Short attention span
- Poor follow-through
- Conflict averse
- Amateurs
- Ideaholics

Preferences
- Stimulate others to think originally
- Support people with innovative notions
- Envision ambitious change efforts
- Reward new ideas
- Conceive significant new ventures
- Design bold organizational initiatives
- Propose dramatic strategies
- Imagine the future
- Moving from company to company in search of new projects and challenges

Typical Work Settings
- Marketing
- New product development
- Strategy
- The arts
- Working for themselves or for a start-up

Figure 2.6. People in the Imagine Profile

management of initiatives, financial measures, acquisitions, marketing, and partnerships—leveraging and extending the products, services, and processes of their firm to increase their value. They judge their success on market share, revenue, brand equity, and profitability.

People in the Improve Profile

People with Improve preferences (Figure 2.8) tend to create incremental results. Though they are capable of moving fast and decisively, sometimes they choose to operate more slowly. They

Positive Characteristics and Types
- Goal oriented
- Action oriented
- Impatient
- Assertive
- Driven
- Decisive
- Challenging
- Tough
- Competitive
- High energy
- Accountable
- High achiever

Preferences
- Model decisive action
- Emphasize goals
- Working their way to the top
- Moving from company to company in search of power and prestige
- Drive for superior returns on investments
- Confront problems as soon as they occur
- Quickly address new difficulties
- Provide fast responses to new issues
- Focus on intended results
- Meet objectives

Negative Characteristics and Types
- Excessive
- Confrontational
- Bossy
- Raging
- Overbearing
- Stressful
- Manipulative
- Workaholic

Typical Work Settings
- Finance
- Brand management
- Mergers and acquisitions
- Investment services
- Managing a start-up

Figure 2.7. People in the Invest Profile

are consistent and methodical producers of optimization and quality through procedures and process improvements. People with Improve preferences are found anywhere that failure is not an option or is expensive, including medicine, engineering, transportation, or military service. Inwardly focused and disciplined, they gravitate toward standardized procedures, rule enforcement, controlled invention, and consistent production. Extensive technology, processes, and systems, such as total quality management and reengineering, are favorites of this profile. Wherever there is complexity, you will find people with Improve preferences.

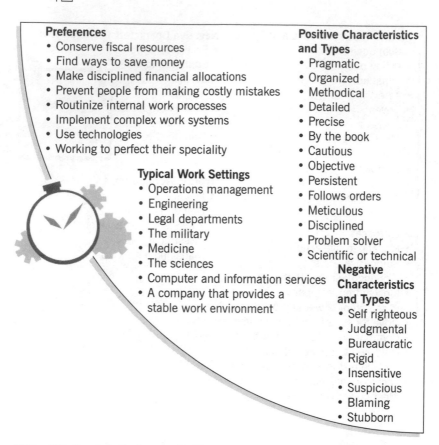

Preferences
- Conserve fiscal resources
- Find ways to save money
- Make disciplined financial allocations
- Prevent people from making costly mistakes
- Routinize internal work processes
- Implement complex work systems
- Use technologies
- Working to perfect their speciality

Typical Work Settings
- Operations management
- Engineering
- Legal departments
- The military
- Medicine
- The sciences
- Computer and information services
- A company that provides a stable work environment

Positive Characteristics and Types
- Pragmatic
- Organized
- Methodical
- Detailed
- Precise
- By the book
- Cautious
- Objective
- Persistent
- Follows orders
- Meticulous
- Disciplined
- Problem solver
- Scientific or technical

Negative Characteristics and Types
- Self righteous
- Judgmental
- Bureaucratic
- Rigid
- Insensitive
- Suspicious
- Blaming
- Stubborn

Figure 2.8. People in the Improve Profile

People in the Incubate Profile

People with Incubate preferences (Figure 2.9) initially create moderate results. While these people will probably take some time to increase their knowledge and skills, once prepared, they can move fast and create big results. They are collaborators who create community and spread knowledge through communication, participation, and learning. Building relationships and empowering individuals is as important to this group as making tangible goods. Customers are like partners in their extended community. Once these internal and external relationships have developed, the resulting informality, self-management, and

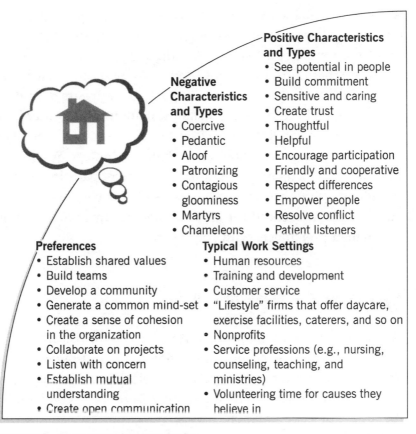

Figure 2.9. People In the Incubate Profile

knowledge may actually increase the speed of new product and service development. In response to uncertainty, people with Incubate preferences foster shared values and goals to provide internal stability and personal growth. They also manage resistance to new ideas by drawing on communication and empathic abilities.

A Caution

Clearly, each profile has distinct tendencies toward particular ways of defining and approaching a problem or an opportunity. Most organizations, however, are a blend of these profiles, both within and across work groups. Likewise, most people are not one type or another and will have at least mild sympathies for other profiles, especially the two that are adjacent to (rather than opposite from) their most dominant profile. Preferences and abilities are also influenced by the situation, so what appears dominant might change from one circumstance to another. Consider how your circumstances influence all the different roles that you play: worker, partner, parent, hobbyist, athlete, volunteer. You have a core, authentic self, but you emphasize different parts in different situations. Ultimately, when you assess the people in your team, you'll want to account for abilities *and* circumstances as you match their preferences with your needs.

■ Assessing Your Creativity Profiles

To use the creativity map in your organization, you'll want to know where you're starting and where you might want to go. You'll also need to consider your capabilities and preferences. The Creativity Assessment in Exhibit 2.2 will help you identify the nature of your situation.

Begin by using the assessment yourself. As you answer the questions, be mindful of your biases. Be very honest with yourself and your organization or department. This assessment is meant to measure your *actual* needs and tendencies, *not your preferences or your ideal situation.* You may find it helpful to take the assessment twice—first to measure your current situation, and a second time, after you read this book, to measure your desired situation.

You will also benefit from gathering perspectives from other people where you work. The assessment can be photocopied and distributed to others in your department or organization. Include people who work beside, below, or above you. Be sure to identify whether you would like them to assess just their department or the entire organization—because these assessments can differ! Consider using the assessment as a basis for group discussion on where you are and where you want to go. Suggestions for analyzing your results and putting them to use follow the assessment itself.

Making Sense of Your Creativity Assessment

When you have completed the Creativity Assessment, plot your scores on the creativity map (Figure 2.10). You can use this map several ways (make as many photocopies of the map as you need):

- Plot your scores for all three parts of the assessment on one map to see how well they are aligned or dislocated. Use different colors to distinguish the purposes, practices, and personal assessments.
- Create three maps, one each for purposes, practices, and person. On each map, plot your scores for both the "current" and "desired" assessments, using two different colors. Compare the results to see where you need to cultivate abilities.
- Photocopy the map onto transparencies, and plot each of the three parts of the assessment on a different map. Gather assessments from other people, and layer up different combinations of transparencies so you can compare the perspectives of a number of people in your department or organization. For example, you might compare how different people assess your purposes or practices at the organizational or departmental level. If there is general agreement, you might want to average the scores for purposes and practices, and (using different colors to distinguish them) compare how the assessments for your department align with the assessments done for your organization as a whole.
- Use the same technique of layering transparencies to compare the range of personal preferences within your department and discuss how well they agree with your departmental purposes and practices.
- Use the same technique to compare the current and desired profiles for your group.

Exhibit 2.2. **Creativity Assessment**

Purposes

This assessment should be used to evaluate the { **current** / **desired** } purpose of your { **entire organization** / **single department** }
(circle one)   *(circle one)*

For each question, rank the four answers according to which is most like your purpose and which is least like your purpose. A rank of 1 means that this characteristic *best* describes your purpose. A rank of 4 means it *least well* describes your purpose. Total each column, and then subtract your totals from 25 to obtain your final score for each profile.

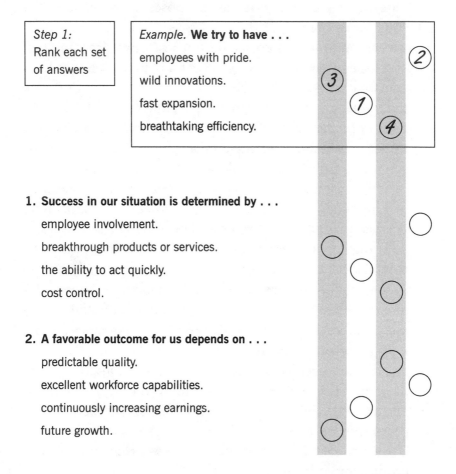

Step 1:
Rank each set of answers

Example. **We try to have . . .**

employees with pride.

wild innovations. ③

fast expansion. ①

breathtaking efficiency. ④

② (for employees with pride)

1. Success in our situation is determined by . . .

employee involvement.

breakthrough products or services.

the ability to act quickly.

cost control.

2. A favorable outcome for us depends on . . .

predictable quality.

excellent workforce capabilities.

continuously increasing earnings.

future growth.

Exhibit 2.2. **Creativity Assessment, Cont'd**

3. Our primary goals are . . .

fast delivery.

radical innovation.

an optimal use of resources.

a loyal community of employees.

4. Our idea of a successful outcome requires . . .

market expansion.

a low rate of errors.

up-to-date workforce abilities.

a profitable bottom line this quarter.

5. A result that we value is . . .

long-range development of our people.

meeting short-term financial goals.

making a dramatic change in our market space.

continuous improvement of our systems.

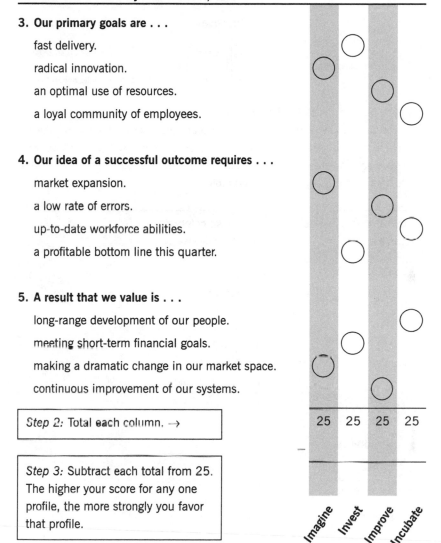

Step 2: Total each column. →	25	25	25	25

Step 3: Subtract each total from 25. The higher your score for any one profile, the more strongly you favor that profile.

Imagine Invest Improve Incubate

Source: From *Creativity at Work* by Jeff DeGraff and Katherine A. Lawrence. Copyright © 2002 by John Wiley & Sons.

Exhibit 2.2. **Creativity Assessment, Cont'd**

Practices

This assessment should be used to evaluate the $\left\{ \begin{array}{l} \textbf{current} \\ \textbf{desired} \end{array} \right\}$ practices of your $\left\{ \begin{array}{l} \textbf{entire organization} \\ \textbf{single department} \end{array} \right\}$
(circle one)   *(circle one)*

For each question, rank the four answers according to which is most like your practices and which is least like your practices. A rank of 1 means that this characteristic *best* describes your practices. A rank of 4 means it *least well* describes your practices. Total each column, and then subtract your totals from 25 to obtain your final score for each profile.

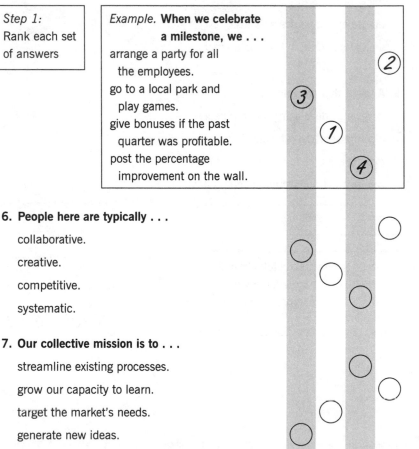

Step 1: Rank each set of answers	*Example.* **When we celebrate a milestone, we . . .**		
	arrange a party for all the employees.		②
	go to a local park and play games.	③	
	give bonuses if the past quarter was profitable.	①	
	post the percentage improvement on the wall.		④

6. People here are typically . . .

collaborative.

creative.

competitive.

systematic.

7. Our collective mission is to . . .

streamline existing processes.

grow our capacity to learn.

target the market's needs.

generate new ideas.

Exhibit 2.2. **Creativity Assessment, Cont'd**

8. **We are good at . . .**

   meeting challenges.

   experimenting.

   administrating.

   empowering people.

9. **We face a problem by . . .**

   brainstorming solutions.

   evaluating our systems.

   training people.

   acting quickly.

10. **We are most likely to conclude a project by . . .**

   sharing what we have learned.

   deciding whether the project met performance goals.

   brainstorming about the next project.

   reviewing how we can make our procedures better
   next time.

Step 2: Total each column. →

| 25 | 25 | 25 | 25 |

Step 3: Subtract each total from 25. The higher your score for any one profile, the more strongly you favor that profile.

Imagine   Invest   Improve   Incubate

Source: From *Creativity at Work* by Jeff DeGraff and Katherine A. Lawrence. Copyright © 2002 by John Wiley & Sons.

Exhibit 2.2. Creativity Assessment, Cont'd

Personal

This assessment should be used to evaluate your $\left\{ \begin{array}{c} \textbf{current} \\ \textbf{desired} \end{array} \right\}$ personal profile.
(circle one)

For each question, rank the four answers according to which is most like you and which is least like you. A rank of 1 means that this characteristic *best* describes you. A rank of 4 means it *least well* describes you. Total each column, and then subtract your totals from 25 to obtain your final score for each profile.

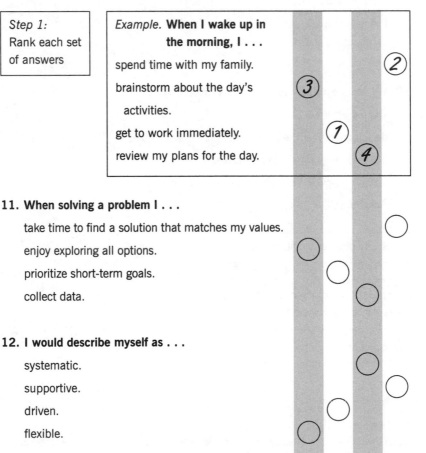

Step 1: Rank each set of answers	*Example.* **When I wake up in the morning, I . . .**

Example. **When I wake up in the morning, I . . .**

spend time with my family.

brainstorm about the day's activities. ③

get to work immediately. ①

review my plans for the day. ④

②

11. When solving a problem I . . .

take time to find a solution that matches my values.

enjoy exploring all options.

prioritize short-term goals.

collect data.

12. I would describe myself as . . .

systematic.

supportive.

driven.

flexible.

Exhibit 2.2. Creativity Assessment, Cont'd

13. I work on projects that . . .

will be completed quickly.

let me invent something new.

create practical improvements.

I can learn from.

14. As part of a team, I bring an ability to . . .

change direction as needed.

keep focused on our process.

foster communication.

get the job done.

15. The most important part of my job is . . .

working with others.

focusing on a specific objective.

thinking up new possibilities.

making systems run smoothly.

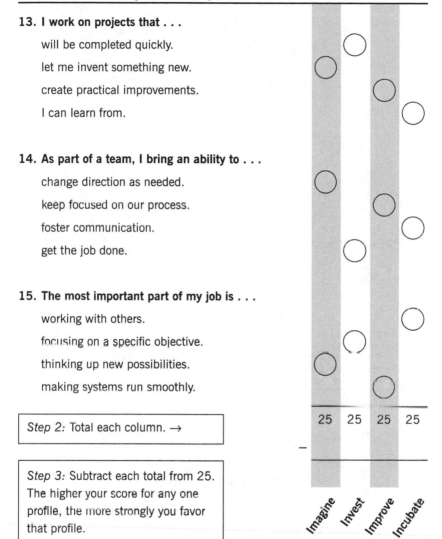

Step 2: Total each column. →

25 25 25 25

Imagine Invest Improve Incubate

Step 3: Subtract each total from 25. The higher your score for any one profile, the more strongly you favor that profile.

Source: From *Creativity at Work* by Jeff DeGraff and Katherine A. Lawrence. Copyright © 2002 by John Wiley & Sons.

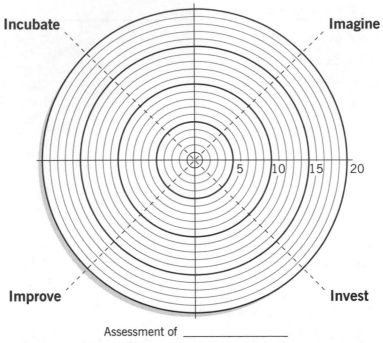

Incubate

Imagine

5 10 15 20

Improve

Invest

Assessment of _____

Use this map to plot the results of your creativity assessments. Mark your scores for each profile on the diagonal dotted line, and then connect the points to form a four-sided figure. (See example.) The resulting figure shows which direction your preferences lean. Use different colors to distinguish your purposes, practices, and personal assessments or to distinguish the assessments from different people.

Example of creativity map with assessment:

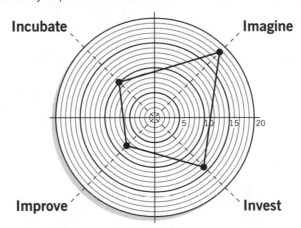

Figure 2.10. Map of Your Creativity Assessment

Source: From *Creativity at Work* by Jeff DeGraff and Katherine A. Lawrence. Copyright © 2002 by John Wiley & Sons.

Alignment of Purposes, Practices, and People

Recognizing whether individual and departmental or organizational profiles are aligned—with each other and with the organization's purposes—can help you to develop the right blend of creativity practices to suit your situation. The results for your assessment suggest how you or your group solve problems, and you may find that you need to shift parts of your profile—by hiring new people, developing useful practices, or changing your purposes—to successfully reach valuable outcomes.

By looking at the overall shape of your profiles, you can see whether you and those around you tend to emphasize certain kinds of purposes, practices, and personal work activities. High scores in more than one profile may mean that you emphasize different profiles at different times. More important, the gaps between profile scores for different parts of the assessment identify what purposes and practices you might want to emphasize or deemphasize. Notice where your purposes, practices, and people align and don't align Alignment among the parts of the assessment shows that your profiles, practices, and people are in harmony, which can be very desirable. However, such alignment may also cause you to struggle if the circumstances change, requiring you to shift your purposes and consequently your practices and people. In contrast, a strategy of intentionally diversifying your profiles—which may, at first, appear to be misalignment—may produce a healthy balance of capabilities. There is no one right solution, but these maps will help you begin to see how to develop creativity in your organization given your circumstances.

As you look at your creativity maps, consider (and discuss with others) the following questions at various levels—as they apply to yourself, to your work unit, and to your organization—depending on what combination of assessments you have done.

General questions
- Who are we? Whose assessments are we considering here, and should they be evaluated as a group? Are there people or units who should be distinct from this group?
- What overall picture of our creativity emerges from the assessment?
- To what extent does our (my) overall assessment align with the purposes of the organization? With its practices?
- How does our (my) profile compare with those of other functional areas or business units?

Purpose questions
- What is our main purpose?
- To what extent do we share the same purpose? Who does and does not share the same purpose?
- What other purposes do we have?
- What are the trade-offs in pursuing these purposes?

Practices questions
- To what extent are our practices aligned with our purposes?
- To what extent are our practices aligned with the purposes of the business unit of which we are a part? Of the organization as a whole?
- How will we acquire, develop, or change practices to help us achieve our purposes?
- Do we have the competencies and culture to develop these practices?

Personal questions
- To what extent is my profile aligned with others in my group?
- To what extent is my profile aligned with the purposes of my group?
- To what extent is my profile aligned with the practices of my group?

- How will I develop and use my skills to work better with the purposes, practices, and people in my group?

Follow-up questions
- If our purposes, practices, and people are aligned, what would happen (both good and bad) if they were *not* aligned?
- If our purposes, practices, and people are *not* aligned, what would happen (both good and bad) if they *were* aligned?
- How will we (I) develop and use our (my) skills to work better with the other practices and people in our organization?

Some groups, particularly within departments or units, may not be pursuing the same purposes as the rest of the organization. Even individual people can be misaligned with the dominant organizational or departmental practices, causing conflict, competing activities, and unintentional hindrances. This misalignment can be good, however, if it creates balance. Our discussion of creativity practices in Chapters Three through Six will assume that the organizational and individual preferences—along with their purposes—are aligned and in agreement. In Chapter Seven, we will explain how these relationships can be considerably more complex and suggest how you can make the most of both alignment and diversity.

CHAPTER SUMMARY
The creativity map applies to purposes, practices, and people. Additionally, it can be used to understand creativity at the level of organizations, units within organizations, and individuals. What is valuable about creativity depends on your perspective, and the purposes pursued by any organization may change over time because these purposes are shaped by both external and internal forces. External forces include both subtle or dramatic changes in the broad commercial environment. Internal forces are shaped by organizational characteristics and values. These forces may constrain or enable a firm as it tries to achieve its purposes.

The underlying theoretical framework of the creativity map helps to explain relationships and tensions among the four profiles. Two main dimensions shape each profile: *focus* (internal versus external) and *approach* (divergent versus convergent). The combination of these dimensions produces two secondary dimensions of creativity: *magnitude* (big versus small) and *speed* (fast versus slow). Imagine practices are externally focused and produce big, breakthrough results with a divergent approach. Invest practices are externally focused and quickly produce results with a convergent approach. Improve practices are internally focused and produce small, incremental results with a convergent approach. Incubate practices are internally focused and produce results with a divergent approach that tends to be slower at first but faster once developed.

For individual persons, the creativity profiles reflect preferences that may or may not match actual abilities. These preferences might also shift according to the roles we play and the people with whom we work. Accounting for both abilities and circumstances is important when matching preferences with needs.

The Creativity Assessment allows you to evaluate and compare purposes, practices, and personal profiles, on your own or across your work group, department, or organization. Discussing these results can help illuminate the ways in which alignment or diversity might be affecting your ability to achieve creative results.

Imagine Practices

Breakthrough Creativity Through Jump-Starting and Forecasting

The Imagine profile is about breakthrough ideas and visions of the future. This is where the most transformational creativity occurs, compared to the other profiles, which tend to be more stabilizing. This approach is most suitable when the situation calls for generating divergent ideas to meet an externally produced challenge or opportunity. Initiating revolutionary creativity practices typically involves high risk and high reward. The risk in this situation is making something that is not different enough from existing options or failing to see a future market opportunity. The rewards are innovation or growth.

Generally speaking, Imagine practices are more likely to succeed when an organization or a work unit is either outperforming expectations or when it is in crisis. In both of these situations, the potential rewards justify the risk necessary for dramatic change. The chief problem with attempts to use these practices is that too often organizations try them in units that are maintaining their equilibrium effectively by using practices that avoid extreme change or risk. Imagine practices make sense when a company is extraordinarily successful because it has the financial buffer to test radical ideas and risk failure, but more important, it has to stay ahead of the pack and continue to outdo itself through reinvention. At the other extreme, when a company is in crisis, any possible success is better than certain death. Start-ups exemplify these dynamics because they inherently operate at the extremes of risk and reward. Consequently, they tend to have more breakthrough creativity than incumbent firms but also a higher rate of failure.[1]

Breakthrough creativity typically requires that you move through one or more complete cycles of speculation, experimentation, and failure in order to explore the boundaries of possibility. To spur innovation or growth, you temporarily take on heightened risk as you try new and different ideas and practices. The key is not to avoid this cycle but rather to accelerate it so as to intentionally learn from your mistakes. This is true for both of the Imagine practices introduced in this chapter: jump-starting and forecasting.

Capsule Overview: Jump-Starting

What jump-starting is . . .
A quick, employee-driven method for
creating radical new products, services, or processes.

Jump-starting encourages wild or breakthrough ideas by bringing together a diverse group of people who want to solve a challenge. They generate new ideas through exposure to a variety of stimuli and hands-on involvement with the challenge. Eventually, they develop criteria for selecting the best ideas and solicit the support of key stakeholders. Learning through trial and error is key to the method.

What jump-starting gets you . . .
Breakthrough products, services, and processes.

Jump-starting is invigorating. Use it to generate group excitement and involvement. It is good when you want immediate breakthroughs and highly differentiated products and services, which bring relatively higher margins.[2] Jump-starting encourages "failing often in order to succeed sooner."[3]

What jump-starting doesn't get you . . .
Low-risk improvements.

The ideas that result from a jump-start process will not produce sure-fire results guaranteed to align with your company's strategic vision or plan. Instead, many of them will be pie-in-the-sky ideas that cannot be manufactured or are not viable from a financial perspective. If you need to extend or leverage your existing technologies or production methods, it is better to plan than to jump-start.

When jump-starting works best . . .
The firm is in crisis or is outperforming expectations.

If you need amazing ideas for new or radically improved products, services, or processes, jump-starting is ideal. Jump-starting is an excellent way to create radical solutions for well-defined problems. If the problem isn't well defined, you'll produce a lot of unrelated or irrelevant ideas. The caveat is that your team must be capable of doing the jump-start process. This means that you should have people who can address both invention and implementation issues (in many cases, this implies a cross-functional team).

Case Study: Success Is More than a Fluke

What kind of company has no obvious business strategy and no dominant core product but has emerged as a world leader in its field? Back in the early 1990s, Fluke Corp.—a test and measurement instrument company—was floundering.[4] Sales had gone flat. The new CEO, Bill Parzybok, thought that he might revitalize the company by narrowing its mission to handheld diagnostic devices. Today Fluke specializes in manufacturing, distributing, and servicing handheld testing and monitoring equipment for technicians, engineers, meteorologists, and computer network professionals. But what truly moved Fluke ahead was its deceptively simple approach to developing new products—it treated the real world as a lab.

One of Fluke's first real-world problems was that computer network technicians could not easily diagnose whether problems were a result of cables, servers, or software. Fluke responded by sending people to spend time with the technicians and determine exactly what was going on. They saw a need for a portable device that would pinpoint the source of a problem. Within a year, Fluke launched a product for testing cables. It worked like a charm. This is now how Fluke translates problem solving into new product development. Fluke went on to develop similar meters for cars, copiers, and elevators.

How does a company promote and sustain this level of innovation? Fluke does so through what it calls "Phoenix teams." To solve a specific client problem, Fluke pulls together a six-person team from the engineering, marketing, and finance departments and jump-starts the creativity process. Participants are selected not for their knowledge of a specific technical issue, but rather for their general curiosity and creativity. (According to Fluke, sometimes expertise gets in the way of fresh thinking.) They are given a hundred days and $100,000 to go into the field and solve the problem. As the project unfolds, the team members learn what they need to know across disciplines. The Phoenix team members immerse themselves in their project, even locking themselves into a "war room" for days so as to avoid all distractions. The team has to observe a strict deadline and budget but enjoys total autonomy in developing several solution proposals. Indeed, Fluke does have an operative business strategy: to leverage problem-solving scenarios into new products and services—continuously.

The Phoenix formula is straightforward: good people are treated like business owners—or rather, problem owners—and encouraged to create solutions that are both novel and useful. It works, too. Since the birth of the Phoenix teams, Fluke has introduced a dozen new products per year, with new products making up 40 percent of overall revenues, and the company's stock price has surged.

■ Discussion: Inspiration Through Disruption

The jump-start approach that Parzybok used to reinvent Fluke can be helpful for any company that is trying to invigorate the creative process. Fluke needed an overhaul and might have suffered a slow death if Parzybok had let the firm continue along its path.[5]

To move itself out of complacency, a company needs to destroy core processes and invent new ones. With each experiment, the company tests the boundaries to determine what is acceptable. Fluke, for example, started its Phoenix teams in response to flagging performance, but the momentum of change continued. The jump-start began with the innovation process, but jump-starting is now a part of the everyday fabric of the firm. These changes forced the company to develop new habits in every way, including work roles, ownership, and leadership.

Work roles. Managers are good at controlling processes but not necessarily good at expanding creative efforts. A company that relies on a hierarchical structure tends to make incremental innovations, creating only within the limitations of its operating processes. In contrast, Fluke needed breakthrough innovations that met undefined needs. By decreasing or eliminating bureaucratic structures, Fluke improved the ability of its employees to connect with key opportunities and with each other. The Phoenix teams helped focus people on their relationship to products rather than to their role or level in the organization.

Ownership. When every person is connected in a hands-on way to a project, the end product is transformed from something abstract and distant to something tangible in which individuals take ownership. By pulling the team away from the hubbub of the company's home base and allowing a solution to emerge, Fluke helped the Phoenix team members invent a solution they truly owned.

Leadership. Since there are few controls in the Imagine profile, the role of the leader is both crucial and unconventional. The real danger is that creativity will not be radical enough. Keeping the organization on the right side of chaos while testing the boundaries of what is possible is a difficult task. The leader has to create a sense of destiny, energy, and fun to motivate the workforce. Jump-start leaders must make sure that they understand the issues work groups face and demonstrate their support for failure. At Fluke, Parzybok introduced a narrowed vision that committed the firm to a particular type of product. However, how to meet that mission was completely negotiable and likely to change. Instead of urging caution in his Phoenix teams, he demanded fresh ideas.

■ Using Jump-Starting: Stimulating New Connections

Breakthrough creativity will not come from walking on the well-traveled path of your company's history. Jump-starting requires changing systems: planning, measuring, designing, financing, marketing, manufacturing, and hiring. Sometimes the first step to creating is by starting from scratch.

This breakthrough strategy is not suited for a stable company with a solid market share that needs to be protected from competitors, unless it can be introduced in a smaller part of the organization that is in crisis or performing exceptionally well. Otherwise, healthy operating units will resist these changes because the intervention will impair existing business structures and efficiencies. It is almost impossible to "destroy" the firm and sustain established, effective systems at the same time. However, sometimes senior leaders will elect to create a crisis in an effort to jump-start their firm out of mediocrity. Without this, radical innovation is likely to succeed only at the margins of the firm, where change is possible and policies and procedures are not entrenched. It is usually easier to change 20 percent of the firm by 80 percent than it is to change 80 percent of the firm by 20 percent.

Using jump-starting to create a wild and freewheeling experience requires some careful thought and planning. As you initiate jump-starting at your organization, pay careful attention to the environment, people, and processes. Remember that jump-starting processes are intense, and pacing is essential to avoid burnout. Moreover, one cannot expect inspired ideas on demand. Optimal experiences for peak creativity—called *flow*—depend on the union of well-matched goals, abilities, and concentration.[6] Self-consciousness can make it hard to achieve such optimal states, and pressure can create discomfort, distraction, or resentment. You must be vigilant for good ideas when they occur rather than forcing them to happen. You need to facilitate breakthrough ideas by focusing on environment, group design, and problem definition.

Environment

Your team will need the space and freedom to create. Help them along by creating a stimulating environment. Use games and physical activities to energize the participants. Sensory stimulation—images, music, textures, scents, and flavors—can help elicit connections between the mind and the physical world. Fun and pleasure tend to coincide with the flow experience, which is the goal of a jump-start brainstorming process.

Often the best way to jump-start a new idea is to leave the office and work with potential clients because they will offer a new context for generating ideas. Similarly, many companies visit specialized jump-starting facilities such as the Eureka Ranch in Cincinnati, Ohio, or the knOwhere Store in Palo Alto, California, to challenge conventional thinking, develop teamwork, and energize the group. Such an off-site, facilitated excursion allows the group to escape the bounds of their usual work setting. The Eureka Ranch crafts a dynamic environment in many different ways.[7] Its staff employs a process that focuses a person or group on a problem and introduces diverse and disorienting stimuli and activities that force new associations. These new ideas can then be developed into practical concepts through trial and error. Although facilitators can be helpful at the start, eventually the team members become trained to run a jump-start on their own.

Group Design

Carefully consider the group of people who participate in a jump-start effort. Typically, small groups are more effective at generating ideas because a tight-knit group will have a greater sense of ownership, and members are more likely to have a closer connection with the group experience, improving rapport and helping ideas to flow. Smaller groups also make things happen because they are not bogged down by size. If jump-starting took place in a larger R&D unit, it might take forever.

Good ideas come when there is a tension created by different perspectives about the task, so this should be a goal when you select people to participate.[8] Whenever possible, choose the participants to bring functional diversity to the team, and when you let them loose, make sure their style of interaction encourages new ideas, because conflict about the process is not helpful. (This doesn't mean that everyone needs to get along, but they do need to be able to create healthy tension and solve it creatively.) Specialists may be particularly useful at certain points in the jump-start process, involved with the group for a specific period of time. For example, content experts can provide a quick and easy source of information about a problem, and jump-start facilitators can inject energy into the group or guide the participants through a sequence of jump-start steps.

Problem Definition

A common mistake in the jump-start process is incorrectly identifying the problem to be solved or the challenge to be met. At Fluke, Parzybok saw that the problem was not about making the company's existing products better; the problem was about discovering client needs. Once Fluke identified the correct problem and outcome, the company could move ahead to generate ideas and select appropriate solutions.

One way to identify the right problem is to keep asking *why*, like a small child. Why do we have this problem? Why is that?" Sometimes, seeing the source of the problem is difficult because our perspective is too close. Have you ever received sage advice from a stranger on an airplane? You've poured out your troubles, and this stranger turns to you and says the most insightful thing you've ever heard. The stranger's secret is having enough distance from your situation to see what is at stake, while you are too close to see the big picture. Some companies get this kind of distance by bringing in an expert in jump-start facilitation or by appointing someone to that role. Whatever approach you take, once you choose the right problem statement, jump-starting can proceed.

■ Tool: Jump-Starting ■

Desired Outcomes
- Generate breakthrough ideas quickly.
- Create energy and fun.
- Transform winning ideas into new initiatives, products, or services.
- Challenge institutional thinking and boundaries.

Time Needed
- Planning and setup: One day (or more if you are arranging an elaborate environment or need to connect with outside clients).
- Sessions: Half-day to full day. You might want to plan a sequence of jump-starting days.
- Frequency: As needed to spur ongoing innovation.

Setting
- Find a place where the group is away from the distractions of an ordinary business day, such as the phone or e-mail. A large room with smaller breakout spaces is desirable. Make sure there are lots of breaks for fun and games, and plenty of creature comforts (good food, congenial music, scenery, pleasant temperature). Encourage casual dress.

Materials
- Lots of flip charts, sticky notes, markers, toys, records, and videos are helpful. Web access and computer projection can help.

Who Should Participate
- Invite up to fifteen or twenty people from diverse backgrounds, departments, and thinking styles. Emphasize the importance of differences. Ask all team members to suspend their voice of judgment.
- You may want to divide a large group into smaller breakout groups of five to six people. The breakout groups can reconvene periodically to share progress.

Facilitation
- Bring a small group of facilitators trained in jump-starts to help with the breakout groups. This is especially important if your company is unfamiliar with the process. If possible, bring in a graphic designer with a computer to create mock-ups of ideas.

Steps of the Process

Brainstorm Possible Challenges
- What's the challenge? Is it to create something new or to solve a problem? Identify several key issues that may be root causes of the challenge.

■ Tool: Jump-Starting, Cont'd ■

Identify the Key Problem
- Write a challenge statement that clearly articulates the challenge to be solved.
- Make sure the challenge is within the means of this group to solve. If not, shrink the challenge or divide it into manageable pieces.

Collect Data
- What do we know? What do we need to know? Who knows what? Gather some facts, information, and opinions on the challenge.
- Consult people with experience and knowledge in this area in order to help the group quickly gather facts and insights and identify land mines and tricks of the trade.

Generate Ideas
- Generate as many ideas as possible in thirty minutes. Write every idea on a sticky note and post them all on a wall where everyone can see them. The greater the volume of ideas and the crazier the ideas are, the better the end result will be.
- Keep in mind some basic guidelines for brainstorming. Design firm IDEO, a champion of brainstorming, uses these rules:[9]
  - One conversation at a time.
  - Stay focused on the topic.
  - Encourage wild ideas.
  - Dofor judgment.
  - Build on the ideas of others.
- When you run out of ideas, use the CREATE and CRITIQUE trigger questions (listed in Exhibit 3.1, at the end of this Tool section) with your idea to boost your output. Add your own ideas to these lists of trigger questions. Ask yourself, "What if we did _____ with this challenge?"
- Time permitting, generate analogies by creating a list of nouns (things). Take the challenge statement and ask how is the challenge like the thing. For example, "How is holiday shopping like a toothbrush?" (or a fish, a typewriter, a first kiss, spring turning into summer, and so forth.)
- Reviewing your ideas, identify those promising the greatest problem breakthrough. Feel free to combine interesting ideas or add new ideas.

Develop Criteria for Success and Select the Most Important Measures
- Value: Is the payoff big enough?
- Cost: Can we afford this?
- Utility: Can it be used in other situations?

■ Tool: Jump-Starting, Cont'd ■

- Feasibility: Can we really do this?
- Time: How long do we have to do this?
- Interest: Who cares?
- Ownership: Who will champion this?
- Immediacy: Is this urgent?
- Direction: Does this fit with our strategy?
- Knowledge: Do we know how to do this?
- Culture: Does this fit with our values?
- Other: Make your own criteria

Select the Best Solutions
- Rank your ideas according to each of the criteria you have selected as important.
- Look at your ranked lists and select the ideas that ranked highest on the most criteria. These are the ideas you should develop further.
- Keep the challenge statement in mind. Work toward a feasible solution, and be objective and willing to confront difficult implementation issues.

Gain Acceptance for Ideas
- Identify key stakeholders—people in your organization who can make this idea happen or stop it from happening.
- Evaluate what they will gain and lose from further implementation of the idea.
- Follow an acceptance-gaining process:
  - Communication: Have you adequately listened to stakeholders' concerns (especially from those who are likely to resist)?
  - Participation: Have you asked important people to join your team? (This helps to alleviate the "not invented here" syndrome.)
  - Facilitation: Have you invited an impartial third party to help mediate differences?
  - Negotiation: Have you considered what the resisters stand to lose by implementing your idea? Can you offer something to offset any losses?
- Create consensus and agreement about next steps and course of action.

Repeat
- If any step doesn't work, go back and try it again until it does. Remind the group that small, temporary failure is part of a successful trial-and-error process. It is not truly a failure if you learn something.

■ Tool: Jump-Starting, Cont'd ■

Exhibit 3.1. Trigger Questions

If your best ideas are not sufficiently better or new, try diverging and expanding possibilities by asking the following CREATE questions:

Combine: What if we combined this with something else?

Reverse: What if we did the opposite?

Expand: What if we made it larger?

Adapt: What if we changed some part of this?

Trim: What if we made it smaller?

Exchange: What if we traded places with something else?

If your best ideas are not sufficiently feasible, try converging and focusing ideas by asking the following CRITIQUE questions:

Credibility: How would we get stakeholders to believe we have what it takes to pursue this idea?

Resources: What money and other resources are required to pursue this idea?

Interest: What do we personally want from pursuing this idea?

Time: What are the time lines for pursuing this idea?

Information: What facts and data should we apply to this idea?

Qualifications: What expertise do we have to pursue this idea?

Understanding: What do we know about this idea? (Apply the familiar newspaper questions: who, what, where, when, why, and how.)

Effect: What result will this idea produce?

Source: From *Creativity at Work* by Jeff DeGraff and Katherine A. Lawrence. Copyright © 2002 by John Wiley & Sons.

Capsule Overview: Forecasting

What forecasting is . . . A process of envisioning
the future and creating opportunities for growth.

Forecasting begins with recognizing emerging trends and forces that are likely to shape future business opportunities. By assessing how these opportunities might affect your business, you can develop a process for updating your firm's strategic approach. Like jump-starting, this process requires iterations of speculation and testing, drawing on the imagination and expertise of your workforce and others.

What forecasting gets you . . .
Commitment to an ever-developing, shared vision.

Forecasting is meant to help you take action. Use forecasting as an ongoing real-time process that will help you shape your strategy, your values, and a vision that everyone can share. Through repeated imagining and testing, you'll keep track of where you are going.

What forecasting doesn't get you . . .
Guaranteed plans in advance.

Forecasting is a divergent practice, encouraging imaginative visions of the future. Consequently, the results of this process will not necessarily align with all the divisions of the company and their associated needs. For example, manufacturing or marketing may not have the kind of advance notice they prefer. You will not be able to plan procurement of resources as precisely as you would like or need to do. Some aspects of your industry or business need to have experts to guide the strategy. If you need to plan for certain processes or if your industry is highly technical, it is better to employ the efforts of strategic planners.

When forecasting works best . . .
Your firm needs everyone to look ahead.

When you expect discontinuous change or innovations in your industry, forecasting can help you anticipate them. It is important to have employees who are capable of extending their imaginations toward future possibilities. The biggest problem of most strategic plans is that they do not gain employee acceptance. By contrast, forecasting engages your employees, helping them endorse and support your company's future directions. When future directions are critical to a company's success, regular use of forecasting can help keep the company on track.

Case Study: Reuters Captures Its Strategic Vision

Like Atlas bearing the weight of the world, the venerable English firm Reuters found itself burdened by a traditional product in a changing market that was rapidly breaking with all conventions. Since its founding in the mid-1800s Reuters had established itself as a giant in the news industry, particularly as a provider of financial information to hundreds of thousands of corporate subscribers worldwide.[10] But with the advent of the Internet, news had become a commodity available everywhere. Reuters was no longer anyone's single source of news.

Somehow Reuters needed to see into the future of the information industry and shift its weight accordingly. Who would be the next competitors and customers? What would be the emerging technologies? With a future filled with infinite possibilities, the situation called for forecasting best- and worst-case scenarios and everything in between.

Tom Glocer, CEO of the Reuters America businesses, decided to try something new. At the annual year-end gathering, typically a celebration of the past and discussion of the future, Glocer introduced the process of forecasting.

First, the participants formed breakout teams by business lines so that everyone with a similar expertise was grouped together. Their task as a team was as follows:

- Weave a story in which you describe your current business lines and customers.
- Identify how the product does and does not meet customer needs.
- Address what you think are the opportunity spaces, your strengths and weaknesses, and your obstacles both now and in the future.
- Explain what you believe the Reuters story *should* be.

The teams diligently applied themselves, came up with some straightforward responses, and presented their stories to the entire assembly. Next, they regrouped with a cross-functional mix that drew team members from as many different departments as possible. Their purpose was to evaluate the stories that had just been presented. Without the constraints of being so-called experts, the eclectic teams tackled the staid stories with fresh thinking. They challenged assumptions: do we really need this business line? They questioned improvements: will this be fast enough, new enough? And they made their own recommendations: what if we shut down a currently profitable business line now because we know it will soon be obsolete?

The groups then presented their challenges and their wildly revised story lines. The original team of experts stepped up to respond to the critique: this quirky idea might actually work, that one doesn't have a chance. Out of this give-and-take process grew yet a third story. Glocer listened carefully to the final versions of each story. Upon deciding which story held the most promise, Glocer awarded the responsible team funding that would help make their story a reality.

The dynamics of crafting, challenging, and revising strategic stories through the interplay of diverse groups resulted in a rigorous assessment of the company's present and future. Additionally, having coauthored the company's strategic plan, employees were willing to make a public commitment to producing results. With a clear vision and people behind it, Reuters started moving with sure footing in new directions.

■ Discussion: Planning for Anything

In contrast to typical strategic techniques based on planning, forecasting pushes a company to imagine what no one knows: the future. By relying on its employees' collective expertise, Reuters was able to speculate on where it could be most successful, not just on where it was best positioned to go. The forecasters thought not just about the future of news and information delivery, but also about what Reuters had the capacity to introduce or alter in the way its industry worked.

This technique is divergent at first, imagining whatever might be possible in a world that might be interrupted by unforeseeable events. The participants identify the best- and worst-case scenarios for their company, pushing toward the boundaries of whatever might be possible. Later, the group, reconfigured to reflect multiple areas of expertise, bring the best and worst cases together in a focused picture of what might happen.

Typical planning strategies are convergent and depend on a *continuous future*, that is, one in which the new inventions or directions are predictable outcomes of current technologies and trends through extension or elaboration of existing technologies. It can be guessed through simple extrapolation of present conditions and technologies. For example, cellular technologies are an outgrowth of existing telecommunications technologies of the past decade. Although their technology is more sophisticated than traditional telephones, cell phones are merely more mobile, not different in kind. In contrast, *discontinuous events* are those that are difficult to predict by examining past trends and technologies. For example, the trend of home banking is one that is unlikely to have been predicted from a past in which banks were always places that consumers would visit. In fact, these changes in the market have been immensely disruptive, causing the large, consolidated banks to lose their dominance because consumers—no longer limited by geography—have greater choices about where to put their money. Ultimately, the degree of continuity or discontinuity is from the buyer's perspective: Does this technology or trend substantially change the way the consumer experiences the product or service?

You are probably familiar with many of the convergent planning strategies used in business. Marketing departments often do "SWOT" analyses to ask, "What are our strengths, opportunities, weaknesses, and threats?" Or they might do an analysis of the market opportunities, considering push (what are the emerging technologies?), pull (what are our consumer demands?), and clash (what are my competitors doing?) factors. Another convergent planning strategy is to identify potential extensions to current branding strongholds. Many companies will think about their existing core competencies and how to leverage them into new arenas, whether new offerings, new clients, or both.[11] Each of these planning strategies assumes a predictable future.

Unlike these common planning methods, forecasting seeks to accommodate a discontinuous and uncertain future. They help you figure out what you can or cannot plan for. When you cannot plan, you must experiment your way into the future. The picture of the future will inevitably change as your company moves forward with your strategy, so your vision must also evolve. Drivers of change—compelling forces that can steer the future in new directions—are recognizable in later stages as trends. A divergent, scenario-building strategy also can take into account these drivers of change and trends. For example, we may not be able to predict who will be the dominant force running health care in the future, but it is safe to say that innovations in pharmaceuticals and genetics will drive it. The company that supplies those innovations is likely to dominate the future of that industry.

■ Using Forecasting: Drawing on the Collective Imagination

Forecasting helps a company account for future discontinuous events by tapping in to the mind-power of a diverse group of people. The process of working in groups based on expertise, followed by groups with cross-functional perspectives, encourages the diversity of thought that can be achieved from functional differences. However, bringing different opinions together requires that the participants work extra hard to communicate with each other across specialties. Also, bear in mind that sometimes the use of experts can limit your view, so encourage non-experts to repeatedly question and challenge. Another benefit of forecasting with larger groups of people, from all over the company and beyond, is that organizations using this practice elicit greater buy-in from employees because the employees have created the vision and plan, they know how to execute it, and they will feel responsible for making it work.[12] Moreover, the company can periodically regather the employees to assess and reconfigure their strategy, and these participants will already be familiar with the prior assumptions of their strategic future. Involvement in the company's strategic future is a valuable way to stay on track over the long term.

To help employees shape such a future with even greater commitment requires deep, multisensory immersion in that vision. Forecasting is an experiment that brings together every resource available: hard data, impressions, sensory information, conversations, symbolism, and imagination. Eventually, a strategic forecast emerges. Such intense experiences, fueled by the act of public commitment, help to make the resulting contract more lasting throughout the organization.

Some firms help companies harness the power of a shared, communal experience. For example, Arcturus's "Adventure

Theater" uses sensory stimuli and ritual in exotic locations to help employees truly understand the company's vision and values.[13] As the participants feel, hear, and see their strategic past and future, it becomes real. They are pushed to confront essential questions about who they are, what they believe in, and what it means to them. Words on a page, spoken by some authority within the organization, cannot possibly convey the same authority and resonance. Instead, the interactive experience allows the entire company to build a shared vision that each employee owns because they helped to create it.

Such an experience is very immediate. The people who participate in the Arcturus experience are changed by it. The use of sight, sound, taste, touch, and smell anchors the event and makes it easier to recall. Cognitive anchors help, too. Symbols—flags, heraldry, insignia, rituals, and stories—reinforce the participants' identification with the group's vision. An organization needs such powerful symbolism to motivate a committed workforce. What inspires people is not a plan but a banner, a fight song, a picture—anything that connects with deeper motivations and emotions.

There are disadvantages as well as advantages to this approach. One disadvantage is directly related to the persistence of the experience. Although employees are deeply committed to seeing their strategy in action, they will also find it difficult to unlearn that strategy, even after it is necessary to change. Another downside is that the company may not create a vision that is well aligned with where it is capable of going. Sometimes experts really do know the best things to consider when formulating a strategy. For example, they know what technologies are on the horizon and the broader competitive landscape. Experts may know possible financial consequences, such as whether the company is a target for a takeover if it pursues such a strategy. It is important to include such rigor as part of the journey, but just as jump-starting brings in the authorities at the end of a divergent process, the forecasting technique should save the experts until later.

This technique is also like jump-starting in that the team is trying to envision the future, but in this case, the future of the competitive landscape rather than future new product ideas. Both tools bring together a diverse group of people, but in forecasting, because it scans the internal and external environment, it typically involves the whole company, or at least a large part of it. The advantage of this technique, again, is the diversity of perspectives that can produce greater insight. By pushing the boundaries of what we know, we have the potential to meet the future, face to face.

CHAPTER SUMMARY

The Imagine profile is concerned with creating breakthrough ideas or a vision of the future. The practices are best suited for situations that need divergent ideas to meet an externally produced challenge or opportunity. Through jump-starting and forecasting, companies in this profile hope to achieve innovation and growth.

Jump-starting is a quick, employee-driven method for creating breakthrough products, services, or processes. This allows a team to learn through hands-on trial-and-error experiments. It is best when solving well-defined problems so that the final solutions are appropriate.

Forecasting is a process of envisioning the future so as to create opportunities for growth. It allows a firm to shape its strategy and vision in a way that encourages the entire firm to participate. It is especially helpful for a firm that expects discontinuous change or innovations in its industry and wants to anticipate these changes.

Imagine practices are best used at the boundaries of performance, because they can make the most difference in exceptional or crisis conditions. The greatest risk in Imagine profile situations is not being radical enough. You need to be prepared to take that leap to reap the high rewards.

■ Tool: Forecasting ■

Desired Outcomes
- Identify key drivers and trends that have a high probability of creating future value.
- Assess what impact these drivers and trends might have on the business or key operating units.
- Develop a process for updating foresight continuously.
- Transform this foresight into action.

Time Needed
- Sessions: A day and a half the first time. (You may need to divide this process into separate sessions, especially if you don't have access to data sources or experts.)
- Frequency: At least two times a year to refresh your vision, but it depends on the nature of your industry and how fast it changes. Meet more frequently if your industry changes fast.

Setting
- Find a place where the group is away from the distractions of an ordinary business day, including phone calls and e-mail. A large room with smaller breakout spaces is desirable. Encourage casual dress.

Materials
- Lots of flip charts, sticky notes, markers, industry publications, and futures reports. Web access and computer projection are helpful.

Who Should Participate
- Assemble a cross-functional team or teams from within and outside the firm, including customers, vendors, managers, and staff. Be sure to include both experts and leaders who have some ownership for the outcomes of the business line. The entire company can participate, but you might find it easier to try this the first time with a smaller group of fifteen or twenty people.

Facilitation
- A facilitator should be employed to keep the group energized and on task.

Steps of the Process

Identify High-Impact and High-Probability Drivers
- Pick an aspect of your business to evaluate and a time horizon for evaluating it (say, three years).
- Identify what you sell in this area, to whom, and who else competes in this opportunity space.

■ Tool: Forecasting, Cont'd ■

- Identify the *drivers* (forces that are pushing the future in this opportunity space) that will have a high impact on this business and a high probability of occurring. Drivers include:
  - Competitors (current positioning, strategy, branding)
  - Consumer demand (buying patterns, preferences, demographic shifts)
  - Technology (innovations, standards, R&D)
  - Partnerships and federations (potential mergers, acquisitions, and partnerships)
  - Internal factors (mission and vision, core competencies, and products in the pipeline)

Identify the Existing *Opportunity Space*
- Speculate how these key drivers manifest themselves as *existing* opportunities and challenges to your line of business. For example, a competitor may be able to enter a key market that your business is incapable of penetrating at the present time. Use the opportunity space matrix (Exhibit 3.2).
- Make sense of these opportunities and challenges as a whole. What do they suggest? Are there overarching themes? What do the most important ones mean to your business line?

Identify the Emerging *Opportunity Space*
- Speculate how these key drivers might manifest themselves as *emerging* opportunities and challenges to your line of business within the specified time horizon (say, three years). For example, a new technology may emerge as a radically new product line that your business is currently incapable of producing. Use the opportunity space matrix shown in Exhibit 3.2.
- Make sense of these opportunities and challenges as a whole. What do they suggest? Are there overarching themes? What do the most important ones mean to your business line?

Collect Relevant Data
- Collect multiple sources of data on the existing and emerging opportunity space themes for this business line.
- Sources of existing data:
  - Industry reports
  - Internal data sources (finance, marketing, strategic planning)
  - Supplier and customer-supplied information
  - Publicly available financial reporting information
  - News reports (magazines, newspapers, Internet)
- Sources of emerging data:
  - Futures reports (futurist societies, consulting firms, think tanks)
  - Experts in the field (researchers, consultants, leaders)
  - Start-ups

■ Tool: Forecasting, Cont'd ■

Exhibit 3.2. Opportunity Space Matrix

Speculate how the drivers (forces that are pushing the future in your opportunity space) might manifest themselves as existing or emerging opportunities or challenges to your line of business. Focus on drivers that are most likely to happen and will have the most impact within the relevant time horizon you have chosen.

Drivers	Existing	Emerging
Competitors		
Consumer demand		
Technology and innovation		
Partnerships and federations		
Internal		
Other		

Source: From *Creativity at Work* by Jeff DeGraff and Katherine A. Lawrence. Copyright © 2002 by John Wiley & Sons.

■ Tool: Forecasting, Cont'd ■

Create a Picture of the Future
- Pick the top themes from the opportunity space matrix and connect them to each of the business lines by making a mock-up of the front page of *USA Today* or some other international publication.
- For each business line have two cross-functional breakout groups create the front page of *USA Today* with a publication date three years from the present date, or whatever time horizon the group has selected.
- In headlines, graphics, short stories, bullet points and photos. . .
  - Subgroup 1 will tell the story of how the business line became the most successful in its sector (or geographic location if applicable) because of the firm's ability to accurately see the future first and adjust the firm's current innovation initiatives in order to ride the wave of success. This is a best case.
  - Subgroup 2 will do the opposite. That is, it will tell the story of why—after a long and successful history—the business line failed in the future using the same criteria.
  - The two groups present their stories to each other. Have fun, but the stories should balance imagination with plausibility.
  - Each group will be given a chance to add potential improvement points to the stories of the other groups to make them more viable. This may be done by introducing new and relevant information, an alternative reasoning process, or *wild card events* (events that regularly occur but are seldom considered in planning; see Exhibit 3.3 at the end of this Tool section).

Create a Dialog Around the Vision
- Have the two subgroups go back and improve their front page to incorporate the relevant potential improvement points.
- The two subgroups then work together to create a probable front page that is a composite of the best and worst cases. They will communicate this to the group at large and to the rest of the relevant stakeholders in the organization.

Share the Vision
- Hang the front page in a place where other members of the firm can discuss its meaning and challenge or add to its content. Periodically, the front page should be updated and its accuracy and validity reviewed.
- Have various groups create their own strategic stories and create greater understanding and involvement at all levels of the firm.

■ **Tool: Forecasting, Cont'd** ■

Exhibit 3.3. Wild Card Events

- New technology breakthrough
- Financial disaster
- Flow of information altered
- Work stoppage
- Lack of qualified designers and operators
- Government regulations
- Cost-based competition
- New competitors emerge
- Materials shortage
- Weather calamities
- Disease outbreak
- Large-scale conflict
- Acquisition or merger
- Value chain reconfigured
- Cost shifting
- Loss of key leaders

Source: From *Creativity at Work* by Jeff DeGraff and Katherine A. Lawrence. Copyright © 2002 by John Wiley & Sons.

Invest Practices

Profitable Creativity Through Partnering and Portfolios

T he Invest profile is about turning creativity into action by providing the necessary discipline and resources. This profile requires creativity to produce monetary value while demanding that risks be calculated. Financially driven creativity practices typically involve crafting a winning strategy. This profile's strengths are best suited to situations that need convergent ideas to meet an external challenge or opportunity. The risk in this situation is not moving fast enough or not maximizing the return on one's investment. The rewards are profits or speed.

This profile views all endeavors as a competition in which only the winners survive. To maximize shareholder value, decision makers taking an Invest approach usually tend to avoid big risks. Instead, a company controls its initiatives by measuring, evaluating, and balancing relative risk and reward. Companies in this profile seek to leverage their products and services to make them worth more collectively than they are individually. The two practices discussed in this chapter, partnerships and portfolios, illustrate how companies achieve something better or new through financially driven creativity.

Capsule Overview: Partnering

What partnering is . . . A mutually
beneficial alliance between parties looking
for opportunities to create synergies with others
outside the boundaries of their unit or firm.

What is creative about partnering is that the alliance creates
something that neither party can do individually, such as offering
a bridge to new markets. Today, partnering is more than just the
traditional type of strategic alliance between two companies. Partnerships are growing not only between companies but between
companies and their customers and even groups of customers.

What partnering gets you . . .
A fast road to value.

Partnerships allow each party to connect with new market
opportunities faster and with greater ease than they could on
their own. Through these connections, the value of what is offered becomes greater than if partners acted independently. By
capitalizing on each other's capabilities, reputations, and access
to customers, partners extend their reach and can offer greater
value to the market.

What partnering doesn't get you . . .
Lasting uniqueness and competencies.

If your plan is to permanently differentiate yourself from
your competitors, it makes more sense to work on your own.
Moreover, you cannot create long-term barriers for your competitors through partnerships because competitors could easily
forge comparable alliances. Also, partnering doesn't give you

the chance to develop the competencies that you would develop through the experience of working on your own.

When partnering works best . . .
The parties involved have complementary needs.

Complementary needs might include customers or products that the other partner doesn't have. Partners must recognize and appreciate the advantages that each party brings to the alliance. Also, the opportunity for synergy is greater when the partnership is likely to be the first to move into a specific market. The greater the value of being first to market, the more each partner stands to benefit from joining forces.

Case Study: Partnership as Community

Partnership usually refers to a business-to-business relationship. But Pierre Omidyar transformed the practice of partnering when he crossed the invisible line and partnered with customers.[1] Legend has it that Omidyar first set up the on-line auction network eBay in 1995 to help his fiancée communicate with other collectors of Pez dispensers. He simply wanted to create a space where people with a common interest could trade stuff that was important to them.

Omidyar's network transformed the typical partnership relationship of business to business by recognizing that customers could also be vendors. Practically overnight, eBay became the world's largest on-line trading community. In this setting, both buyers and sellers are simultaneously customers and partners with eBay. Selling and bartering for used merchandise in a common market space represents pure commerce—no products produced or services rendered, only exchanged.

A major lure for eBay's customers is the ease of entry into the partnership. Even for the first-time user, the initiation is painless. A quick briefing of the rules lets you know how to bid, buy, and sell. If you are curious but perhaps a little tentative, you can browse to your heart's content before making a bid. You can peruse categories such as jewelry and breweriana (collectibles for beer aficionados), explore themes such as Elvis and Chinatown, or visit specialty sites such as upscale Sotheby's and the down-home business exchange where companies trade in kind. Finally something catches your eye. It's an old metal sign advertising Guinness, the one your dad's been coveting for years. So now you look into the reputation of the seller. How many prior transactions has the seller completed? What kind of feedback did previous buyers leave about this particular seller? What does the seller have to say about her own business? All this information is a click away.

When your questions and concerns have been sufficiently addressed, you register yourself and go straight to the auction block. The starting bid on the Guinness sign is $29. You are feeling cheap, so you enter your highest bid at $33. eBay then serves as your proxy. If someone else bids $30, eBay will put you in for $31 and so on up to your highest bid. If someone outbids you at that point, you're out of the game. But this time you are in luck. You secure the sign for an affordable $31. The seller contacts you by e-mail regarding payment and shipping details. You pay by money order or credit card. The seller sends you the sign. You and the seller post feedback about your experience on the eBay site. Done deal. And you've made your dad's day.

Like the matchmakers of old, eBay derives its remarkable success from the ability to hook up partners. Unlike conventional firms, however, eBay has partnered not with fellow corporations, but with you, the consumer. Essentially, buyers and sellers do all the work. You negotiate the terms of the transaction. You handle shipping and inventory. For a cut of the seller's price, eBay simply provides the space in which supply and demand meet.

Because of the nominal overhead, eBay reaps phenomenal profits. After the Internet bubble burst in 2000, eBay was one of the very few dot-coms that the market still deemed valuable. Its unique strength comes from the sound partnerships it has forged with a community of people and companies united by shared aims.

■ Discussion: Changing the Interface of Commerce

As the eBay case demonstrates, partnering can be like serving as a broker or aggregator. The broker or aggregator has nothing to sell except its ability to create a network, a system for making connections. The sellers and the buyers are happy to draw on this resource because otherwise they might not meet each other, or at least not easily. Were it not for its partnerships, eBay would be a nonentity. Although eBay's partnerships are not the traditional one-to-one pairing or several-to-several alliance, the opportunities created by eBay and its many partners represent two of the key benefits of partnering: faster access to new markets and learning from others.

New markets, faster. Partnerships allow each of the parties to grow faster and reach new markets more easily than they could on their own. In general, partnerships reduce the typical barriers to entry. eBay fills a gap between two parties who do not know each other and have no way of contacting each other.[2] Sellers use eBay to connect to a number of remote buyers, who come to the site because they know they will find sellers. The greater the number of customers, the greater the incentive to sell or shop on the site.[3] In short, eBay creates markets for its partners.

Learning from others. Partnerships offer the benefits of knowledge through connections. For example, manufacturers and suppliers who develop close ties are better able to exchange resources, learn and devise solutions, and respond quickly to market needs. They share more detailed information with each other, and over time, they can anticipate what each other might need. Indeed, in one study of entrepreneurial firms in the garment industry, partners tended to inform each other when they anticipated future work slowdowns or they would place orders early to improve cash flow for a partner whose business was slow.[4]

Similarly, partnerships help the parties involved have equitable access to new information. eBay is a post-capitalist business model in that information is no longer concentrated in the hands of the few. Because the company is in a partnership with its customers, information is accessible and transparent to all parties. For example, a buyer searching for a particular item can compare prices of all similar items to get a sense of the fair market value. Through the creative use of technology, eBay has redefined business transactions as cooperative rather than competitive.

■ Using Partnering: Focusing on Benefits for All

Partnerships are creative when collectively they produce something new that could not be produced by any one partner individually. For example, most computer manufacturers set the specifications for their suppliers, but Dell Computer Corporation wants the partners that manufacture its component parts to include their latest innovations in what they supply. Instead of conducting its own R&D, Dell uses partnerships to offer state-of-the-art technologies in its computers. In addition, partnerships can create new markets and help bring resources to new ideas that might not otherwise move forward. Here, creativity is in "the art of the deal."

Partnering isn't just for senior leaders with access to vast organizational resources. You can reap the benefits at middle levels of the organization with internal (other teams or departments) or external (other firms, vendors, and even customers) partners. In the best partnerships, businesses and consumers alike achieve results that are more extensive, faster, easier, and lower risk.

Business Benefits

For the businesses involved, the most important benefits of partnerships are extension and speed. Each firm can extend and elaborate its existing products or services in new ways and can extend existing products into new markets. And it can do so more quickly. For example, sales organizations can get to a new market faster when a partner brokers the introduction, as when Disney promotes a new movie through McDonald's Happy Meal prizes. The partnership isn't making the specific products more creative, the creativity comes from the solution that serves both parties' marketing needs.

A third benefit of partnering for businesses is that reaching objectives is easier. For example, in high technology, two pharmaceutical companies can complement each other's gaps in research and development by jointly developing a drug delivery mechanism and individually offering their own drugs through the same mechanism.

Also, each partner increases safety by reducing risk. For example, through a partnership, a company can enter new markets that it could not afford to enter on its own, and it gains the knowledge of how to target consumers in that market appropriately. Collectively, partners attract a wider or more focused audience, which reduces risk.

Consumer Benefits

For consumers, the three principal benefits of partnerships are speed, simplicity, and reduced risk. For example, using the services offered by eBay is a faster way to shop: eBay creates a searchable marketplace directory on-line. The services are easier to use: at eBay, the customer can learn one system for accessing an enormous range of products instead of learning scores of systems at different sites. Finally, eBay is less risky than many kinds of on-line shopping, providing insurance for transactions and verifying the credibility of the vendor. At its best, partnering creates value by being beneficial to all.

Making Partnering Effective

Staying focused on mutual benefits is a key to making a partnership work. As distinct firms, partners will not share every strategic objective, and it would be dangerous to assume that their joint strategy is the same as the individual strategy of either party. Likewise, partners should be willing to rethink and redesign their joint processes repeatedly, remembering that what unites them is the end product and the promise of mutual gain.

In particular, effective partners must work to maintain a good rapport. Rapport can't be bought; it comes through working together and establishing trust. Partners need constant communication because timing is everything when the goal of partnering is to reach markets faster. When opportunities emerge, they can move quickly. The best business partnerships are based on experience and understanding. Each business asks, "What does each of us need, and what can each of us deliver?" The creative part of partnering is finding and selecting synergistic products and services from the pool of resources that they share.

One of the most valuable creative assets for any manager working in the Invest profile is the ability to manage people and resources not under the manager's control. Most people are limited by organizational boundaries, yet partnerships allow everyone to extend these boundaries considerably without requiring vast resources. This tool is designed to help you think about and try the opportunities that partnering offers.

■ Tool: Partnering ■

Desired Outcomes
- Access new markets.
- Reduce time to market.
- Develop new competencies and benefit from other partners' complementary ones.
- Overcome resource barriers.
- Reduce risk.

Time Needed
- You'll need enough time to gather information and then develop rapport with your partner. Arranging partnerships can take a lot of time, but by regularly thinking about potential opportunities, you'll be poised to act fast when necessary.

Setting
- Anywhere in the world there are potential partners. Be prepared to travel.

Materials
- As much information as possible on potential partner firms and markets. Information can be obtained through a combination of public records, indirect information from parties who have a deep knowledge of the potential partner, and direct conversations with the potential partners.

Who Should Participate
- Include members of your unit or firm who possess a deep understanding of the firm's operations and the particular needs that you might have. They should be authorized to make deals.
- Include experts in the type of the deal you want to make.

Facilitation
- The head of the partnership team will depend on the nature of the partnership and the degree of formality with which the partnership is forged.

Steps of the Process

Determine the Needs
- The team should articulate its goals and decide if a partnership is needed or if the goals can be achieved by other means.
  - How do the goals of a potential partnership align with your current strategy?
  - What do you hope to gain from a partnership?
  - What might you lose from a partnership?

■ Tool: Partnering, Cont'd ■

- What are the short-term and long-range effects of the decision to make a partnership?
- What will change when you make a partnership?
- How will you ensure that a partnership runs effectively?
- Identify the "must have" goals and focus on them.

Get Your Facts Straight
- Gather and analyze key information on potential partners:
  - What products do they sell?
  - What are their target markets?
  - Who are their key competitors?
  - Who are their other partners?
  - Do they have the ability to meet their partnership commitments?
  - What are their unique competencies?
  - What is their culture like?
  - What are their strategic aspirations?
  - How well do we fit together?
- Assessing each potential partner's competencies in making, selling, and supporting its products, business lines, and operations is useful, especially as they might complement your own gaps. See Exhibit 4.1 for a selection of capabilities that you might consider.

Exhibit 4.1. Assessing a Potential Partner's Capabilities

Capabilities for Making	Capabilities for Selling	Capabilities for Servicing or Supporting
■ Research, design, and development ability	■ Access to adequate and sustainable markets	■ Supportive organizational culture
■ Protected intellectual property	■ Brand and reputation	■ Workforce and leadership competency
■ Capital for investment	■ Appropriate sales channels	• Fluency in other cultures and languages
■ Supplies	■ Qualified sales agents	■ Product and customer knowledge
■ Development and manufacturing technology	■ Ability to launch a sales campaign	■ Availability of qualified service staff
■ Capacity to meet specifications	■ Marketing budget	■ Resource availability
■ Capacity to manufacture at scale	■ Appropriate product pricing	■ Decision-making authority

---

■ Tool: Partnering, Cont'd ■

Look for Fit
- You want to find partners who complement you by helping you do something you cannot do without them, whether that is creating products, services, or reaching markets. At the same time, even though you may be only partnering in a single area such as research, you will be engaging the entire partnership firm, so other factors will have an impact on your ability to make this alliance work. Look for vision, culture, and processes that are compatible with your own.
  - *Vision:* Identify signs that suggest where a potential partner firm is going: strategy, resource allocation, new products and services, market presence. Also consider how the partner firm is pursuing its vision. For example, is it taking an incremental or breakthrough approach? Is it developing its own competencies or forging multiple alliances? (As a general rule, it is easier for incumbents in a particular market to extend their products incrementally than it is for a new entrant. Conversely, it is typically easier for a new entrant to introduce disruptive breakthroughs into existing and newly created markets than it is for an incumbent because the entrant is not protecting existing market share or technologies.)
  - *Culture:* Look for signs that suggest what a potential partner firm believes and values: language used around the office, observable rituals, use of office space, resolution of conflicts, and how people are promoted or disciplined.
  - *Processes:* Look for signs that suggest where a potential partner firm may have systems and technologies (such as Internet access or CAD/CAM equipment) that you may be able to leverage together to create new products and services.

Select a Partner
- Make a short list of candidates (three at most).
- Choose the first potential partner to approach. (If your first choice doesn't result in an agreement, return to the list, but also reevaluate your criteria to understand whether you need to shift your selection process.)

Initiate an Agreement with a Potential Partner
- Remember not to take so long in your assessment and planning that you never move ahead. Once key potential partners have been identified, determine the key decision makers who can make these alliances happen and meet them.
- Specify the goals of the partnership: target objectives, schedules, revenues, and the like.

■ Tool: Partnering, Cont'd ■

- Although forging a partnership is complex, a few key decisions about the nature of the relationship will make things easier as you go forward:
  - Put the desired goal of the partnership in writing to keep it front and center.
  - Decide who owns what.
  - Specify who is responsible for what.
  - Stipulate who holds liability for what.
  - Recognize each other's intellectual property.
  - Agree on escape clauses.
- After these agreements are established, they can be formalized. Make a formal, mutual commitment to trying to make the partnership work. Agree upon a way to resolve disputes, because they are inevitable. Also, develop a shared managerial process for project management to keep initiatives on track.

Test the Relationship
- Test the partnership with a single initiative if possible. (If the window of opportunity is short, don't waste time testing.) If your partnership works out, expand it to other areas and greater levels of commitment. For example, make a product or service together incrementally, and test it. Discover the opportunities and challenges while learning how to work together Then decide if this arrangement still makes sense as you move toward full-scale implementation.

Source: From *Creativity at Work* by Jeff DeGraff and Katherine A. Lawrence. Copyright © 2002 by John Wiley & Sons.

Capsule Overview: Portfolios

What portfolios are . . .
Collections of initiatives, viewed as investments,
that will become products, services, or companies.

The aim of the portfolio is to compare, balance, and maximize the relative value of these investments through disciplined decision making and resource allocation. Depending upon who holds the portfolio, a portfolio might include entire companies, individual products and services, or projects (such as an internal research initiative).

What portfolios get you . . . A safer path to value.

Portfolios are a good way to make sure that your division or company has an array of offerings that increase rewards through synergy, leveraging, and spreading risk. By imposing thoughtful processes and metrics, you can reduce the risk inherent in creating new products and services. Your resources can be optimally targeted toward the investments that are best for the company's strategic goals.

What portfolios don't get you . . . Flexibility.

Capitalizing on emerging opportunities is nearly impossible in a portfolio system because products are systematically evaluated in stages to minimize risk. This process takes time. Because some opportunities emerge unexpectedly and their time horizons are short, a response must be developed very quickly, making a staged portfolio evaluation process impossible. Thus, companies that rely on portfolios may miss these opportunities rather than take the risk of sidestepping the portfolio process.

When a portfolio works best . . .
Its contents result from a diverse array of
evaluation criteria, such as value, strategic fit, and risk.

Portfolios are useful when product development is complex, technical, or expensive because each product's potential can be evaluated against specific criteria at several points along the way. These evaluations must be able to identify future winners and losers. Portfolios also help to balance long-term and short-term goals along with different levels of risk and reward.

■ The Advantages and Pitfalls of Traditional Portfolio Management

Portfolio systems have two ingredients. The first is the array of projects that are developed and evaluated in the portfolio. (We are using the term *project* broadly.) The second is a "stage-gate" process[5] (also called a *tollgate process*) by which the company monitors each project's viability throughout its development. The money for development is connected to this monitoring process.

Generally, in organizations that run cross-functional project portfolios, management teams make decisions designed to increase the value of the collection of projects while improving time to market and decreasing risk. Some items help to leverage others. For example, a company might sell a less profitable item because it creates demand for higher-profit, related products. Together, the complementary items increase overall value across market segments and product lines.

The projects in these portfolios follow set stages of development such as the following:[6]

- Ideation
- Preliminary investigation

- Detailed investigation (for building a business case)
- Development
- Testing and validation
- Full production and market launch

Portfolio reviews at each stage rely on gathering diverse perspectives about starting new initiatives, making decisions about projects in process, and guiding the creation of new products and the extension of existing ones. The aim of the review gates is to strategically align projects, maximize their individual and collective value, minimize risk, improve the probability of commercial success, and allocate resources according to the company's priorities. Evaluators decide whether a project idea meets the criteria. Although the criteria are different at each stage, they basically address two kinds of questions:

- *Value:* Does this project maximize value for the organization? Is it strategically aligned? Does the project need more or less money for the upcoming stage? Overall, is the portfolio of projects balanced?
- *Progress:* Did the project meet the goals of the most recent phase? Is it likely to meet the goals of the subsequent phases?

The answers to these questions help the review committee determine if the project is aligned with the goals of the company. Typically, the committee answers these questions by using numeric, often financial, ways of assessing the merit of potential projects. Such numeric assessments may include Net Present Value (NPV) and an array of scoring, checklist, ranking, and probability evaluations of particular aspects such as manufacturing feasibility or time to market.[7]

Such a committee can make one of four possible decisions about any given project in the portfolio: stop, go, modify, or put on hold. Stopping projects that do not meet the criteria is key to keeping financial resources fluid so that they can be applied to the best opportunities. Portfolios offer the flexibility to get in and out of projects, keeping options open to real-time strategic changes. Ideally, the cost of development increases only toward the end of the project development cycle, when ideas have been refined to the point of reduced risk. Thus, a good portfolio management company keeps a large number of ideas coming into the stage-gate process and only a few initiatives coming out. Overall, this practice makes the portfolio healthier by committing full resources only to the best ideas.

By using portfolios, companies hope to get greater, more consistent financial returns with less risk. However, traditional portfolio management has four major pitfalls:

- *Creating too few projects.* Portfolios should be a way to explore and review a wide variety of project ideas, but too often the process itself encourages companies to pursue only the ideas that look most likely to flourish. By not exploring a greater number and wider array of ideas, even the ones that might fail, the reviewers miss the opportunity to learn from their initial explorations.
- *Stopping too few projects.* Paradoxically, portfolio reviews can also tend to be too kind. Once a project has made it partway, reviewers are often reluctant to stop investment. They may not know how to evaluate appropriately.[8] Also, reviewers may overvalue the sunk costs or personalize their commitment to the project.[9] Two problems that result: the projects in the portfolio are not truly outstanding, and the company does not have the human or financial resources to pursue each project adequately.[10]
- *Evaluating projects by biased criteria.* Those who guide portfolio management—financially minded members of the Invest profile—bring their biases with them. Their criteria are based on financial returns and are often focused on the short

term. The projects that survive are all geared toward these indicators of success. This is like making a variety of animals pass a flying test. The birds will fly, but the fish won't. Thus projects that develop long-term competencies or radical projects with risk are sacrificed in favor of more conventional, short-term payoffs. Often, portfolios might deprive experimental projects of funding because they don't show promise fast enough.

- *Encouraging short-sighted thinking.* Firms tend to protect the products or projects that are good moneymakers. By focusing other projects toward leveraging the sources of profit, companies fail to look ahead to future developments in their market. As a result, they may get caught off guard by a competitor who invents something more in tune with consumer needs.

To summarize, classic portfolio management involves testing and exploring a diversity of project ideas that are refined down to a select number of valuable offerings. However, portfolios are not always run with a formalized, mathematical template. The following story is about a firm that manages portfolios that includes companies, initiatives, products, and services.

Case Study: A Laboratory for Business Ideas

Bill Gross made a career out of having better ideas—a lot of them.[11] Gross put himself through the California Institute of Technology with money earned from his own businesses selling stereo speakers and parabolic solar reflectors. After college, when he sold a software company he had started to Lotus for $10 million, it was clear that he had a good eye for picking winners. He captured the attention of several investors, including movie mogul Steven Spielberg, Compaq Computer Chairman Ben Rosen, and actor Michael Douglas, who gave him the capital to start a laboratory for building start-ups. The company—called idealab!—would develop mostly Internet-related firms where barriers to entry were relatively low and knowledge management was key.

Founded in 1996 at the dawn of the Internet Age, by the year 2000 idealab! had launched dozens of start-up businesses, including dotTV.com, CarsDirect, Tickets.com, and Citysearch. More important, Gross invented an approach to innovation that would become one of the financial hallmarks of the Internet boom: incubating businesses from a novel idea to an operating entity. One of the unique things about idealab! is that Gross would create an idea, wrap a company around it, and then create products and services within the new company.

Incubators, econets, and accelerators (as they would come to be known) are outgrowths of Gross's concept. Gross developed a replicable and scalable process for creating start-up businesses, offering management and support to a portfolio of new ventures. With a hub-and-spoke setup, the firms shared support services but had separate management. Initially, each start-up venture received relatively little in the way of cash but a great deal in the way of advice: strategic, financial, legal, technical, and general entrepreneurial wisdom from someone who had been through the process before. This approach freed the entrepreneurs from the time drain of handling administrative details and locating lawyers and bankers, allowing them to focus on developing their ideas. Opportunities for buying from and selling to other firms in the portfolio, along with pooling common overhead resources, created additional economic advantages. In return, idealab! held between 25 and 49 percent of the equity when the start-up left the incubator for funding from a venture capitalist or other financial institution.

Gross founded his incubator with some initial rules. He limited cash available at the start, believing that an idea should be strong enough to interest venture capitalists. He also didn't pursue an idea if no one at the incubator was willing to pursue it. Gross relied heavily on his own sense for great ideas and his ability to surround himself with credible experts. What was unique was that this incubation process was more about cultivating winners than eliminating losers. Gross figured that he would learn from his mistakes, and over time, his rules became more fluid in response to his successes.

By early 2000, idealab! had raised more than $1 billion in capital to finance the growth of its incubator. It began to invest heavily in its existing portfolio of ventures along with other businesses outside its umbrella organization. Within eight months it had spent more than $800 million. Then things began to go downhill. In the late spring of 2000, the stock market "corrected," and the Internet bubble popped. Idealab! firms such as eToys, promoted as the business model of the future, began to fail. The press turned contemptuous, labeling incubators as "incinerators" for the way they burned up money. Gross noted that he had strayed too far from his core ability to spot good ideas and nurture each business: "We were acting like VCs without the skill or the interest."[12] Within months he had gone from media hero to the poster boy for everything that was wrong with the "new economy." But in the meantime, Gross had created a highly creative business model that forever changed how new ideas are transformed into commerce.

In the first quarter of 2002, a group of investors filed a lawsuit demanding that Gross dissolve idealab! and return a sizable portion of the $1 billion investment they had made.[13] The investors claimed that Gross mismanaged the company by investing in failing companies and focusing on his personal financial benefit. Idealab! responded that the allegations were incorrect. Whatever idealab's future, this case reinforces important points in this book. As we suggested in Chapter Two, the best person to invent a start-up is not necessarily the best person to supervise the ongoing management of a more mature firm. And as we will now discuss, managing a portfolio requires discipline and diversity, plus insight.

■ Discussion: Portfolio Management as an Art and a Science

Idealab! may have made some mistakes that put its future in jeopardy. But Gross did invent the modern incubator, with a process for portfolio management that took conventional investment principles and stretched them to their boundaries. The strengths and weaknesses of idealab! suggest possibilities for more conventional portfolio management and reinforce the most important components of a portfolio used creatively.

Look for diversity and synergy in developing a portfolio. Each start-up was designed to pursue a focused, niche market rather than be a broad business that would satisfy everyone's needs. Unfortunately, Gross's overall portfolio focused too heavily on e-commerce, and when the technology slump hit, just like regular investors who foolishly put all their stock in one sector, he lost money because he was not buffered by a diversity of initiatives, products, and companies.

Even so, the individual start-ups benefited by being part of a portfolio of Internet technology businesses under the idealab! umbrella. The core of incubator services helped the managers in the individual businesses put their energy into important, core business tasks and save money through economies of scale.[14] By researching available technologies or developing new ones, idealab! did the legwork that saved the start-ups the time of doing it themselves. The incubator eliminated other time-eaters that commonly delay the growth of a new business so that these Internet businesses could launch in record time. In the Invest profile, time makes all the difference.

Get the best advice. From the start, idealab! involved a wide array of high-profile experts such as Spielberg and Rosen, along with Jack Welch of GE, MIT professor Sherry Turkle, Apple Computer graphic designer Tom Hughes, and information architect Richard Saul Wurman. By giving equity to these experts, Gross put himself in a position to solicit their advice. This investor relationship set him up to quickly obtain additional judgments.

Turn experience into informed action. Applying experience was key to Gross's portfolio model. Rather than killing the losers early, Gross focused on cultivating the winners, letting the losers determine their own fate. He accelerated the failure cycle so that he could apply the lessons from his mistakes in the businesses that failed. He did not demand rigorous business models, preferring to change the model over time, and indeed, he discovered some lucrative business plans that way. Gross would even prototype a new business idea on-line to see if the concept worked.[15]

By going through the stages again and again in order to get them right, Gross refined his ability to develop the idealab! portfolio.

Meanwhile, Gross enabled the individual start-ups to observe and exchange ideas with the others going through similar stages.[16] They would see how to avoid mistakes and could jump on emerging opportunities created by other firms. This made the uncertainties of entrepreneurship feel more stable. Moreover, being part of such an environment was attractive to new people interested in managing one of the portfolio businesses.

Establish good criteria and stick with them. In the idealab! model, much of the success of the portfolio was tied up in the art of individuals. Gross's personal talents, combined with the talents and resources of others, were what generated, screened, developed, tested, and launched the portfolio's pieces. There was no formal process by which the portfolio was reviewed as a whole because Gross hoped to learn from his failures. In contrast, the more conventional approach to portfolios is so dependent on metrics and processes that the company may never take risks that allow anyone to learn something new.

Ultimately, good portfolio management happens somewhere in between. It is best to have both process and instincts, relying on the diversity of understanding that comes from reading the numbers and listening to the gut.

■ Using Portfolios: Supporting the Survival of the Fittest

The essence of a great portfolio is that a number of great ideas come together in one place, matching opportunities with solutions.[17] The healthiest portfolios are those that are *challenged* to perform their best by heightening the competitive environment. Portfolio management challenges its holdings through the allocation of resources, reduction of risk, and alignment of values.

An effectively managed portfolio allocates resources in a way that maximizes value for the portfolio as a whole. Even though a product does not promise great profits, it may be the conduit to great profits for another product. The strength of portfolio management as a technique for leveraging creativity is that it puts resources with the best ideas. Diverse criteria that account for multiple perspectives of risk and reward are essential for selecting ideas because they promise diverse portfolio contents.

A portfolio should minimize risk but not always eliminate strange ideas. Risk can also happen when a portfolio has a lot of very safe, homogeneous holdings. Just as with an investor's portfolio, diversity is a better way to minimize risk. Thus it is better to develop a portfolio that can address the multiple directions that the market could take. For example, a pharmaceutical company that begins development of a hundred drugs will make most of its money from just a few of those developed. Even though those few seem like a safe source of income, the company can never tell when one of its star products will no longer be the moneymaker because some other drug replaces it. Therefore, it is important to keep the portfolio developing by adding new projects regularly, making sure that projects are on track, cutting projects that are not strong, and keeping the overall contents diversified.

Portfolios are also designed to help a company keep its focus on its strategic values. Prioritizing needs to be firm and consistent. The key is to use a consistent method to pick winners and avoid losers—and follow it! At the same time, strategic goals may be broader than immediate appearances. For example, in the early 1980s, IBM did not consider personal computers as part of a portfolio of offerings. Consequently, it outsourced its chip making to Intel and its operating system to Microsoft. Instead of developing business lines within a complementary portfolio, IBM handed these opportunities to outsiders.

Essentially, the value of any one end product is determined in the context of the entire portfolio. Portfolio management becomes a creative way to maximize value when decision makers remember that the whole is more than the sum of its parts.

■ Tool: Portfolios ■

Desired Outcomes
- Increase the value of the portfolio of creative initiatives.
- Put the best ideas on a clear and fast track to success.
- Make sure the ideas with most promise get the most resources.
- Align new products and services with strategy.
- Reduce risk by balancing types of initiatives progressing through the portfolio (for example, incremental improvements and breakthrough inventions).

Time Needed
- Sessions: Proportional to the size of the portfolio and the number of holdings.
- Frequency: As appropriate for your development cycle.

Setting
- Meet in a central location in the office, such as a boardroom. Team members associated with specific projects should be on call in case there are technical questions that only they can answer.

Materials
- Financial, market, and project data.

Who Should Participate
- A management team made up of a diversified group of senior leaders, product managers, and technical experts from all the relevant, major business lines and geographies. Portfolio management requires decision making and resource allocation at the highest possible levels of the organization or its business units.

Facilitation
- The head of the portfolio evaluation team should chair this meeting.

Steps of the Process

Determine the Needs
- Determine what outcomes the portfolio process must produce. Consider your purposes! Here are some of the possible goals to consider:
  - Increase the NPV of the portfolio.
  - Reduce cycle time.

■ Tool: Portfolios, Cont'd ■

- Reduce failure rates.
- Align the portfolio with strategic focus.
- Diversify types of innovation, markets, and business lines.
- Leverage innovation across business units and locations.
- Launch higher-impact initiatives.

Establish Reward and Risk Measures and Criteria
- Establish key performance measures to set the level of reward that the portfolio must return and the risk that it will tolerate. Because the Invest profile has a financial bias, it is typical for portfolio managers to skew the portfolio to maximize returns and minimize risk for each individual holding. However, the way to manage risk across the entire portfolio is to diversify the initiatives that it includes.
- Include both qualitative and quantitative measures. Qualitative measures might include peer review, leadership assessment, or customer opinion research. Quantitative measures can evaluate outcomes such as cost or failure rates. Here are some examples of measures:[18]

  Reward Measures
  - Net Present Value (NPV) of each initiative and of the portfolio as a whole
  - Time remaining until commercial introduction
  - Increase in market share
  - Stretch and leverage of existing product lines
  - Degree of product differentiation and diversification
  - Likelihood of gaining internal capabilities by learning from the development process

  Risk Factors
  - Technical gap between current products and target idea
  - Industry and technology standards
  - Technology skill base
  - Market need and demand
  - Competitive landscape
  - Impact of government regulation
- A reward and risk diagram (Figure 4.1) can be used to survey the relative prospects of the initiatives within a portfolio. This tool enables the group to review all initiatives together in terms of their degree of risk and reward so that you can see whether you have an appropriate balance. To do this, you must develop key measures for reward and risk. These measures can be singular or a collection of measures that add up to a single number. Place these initiatives on a graph like Figure 4.1, marking each initiative with a circle proportional to the size of your investment.

■ **Tool: Portfolios, Cont'd** ■

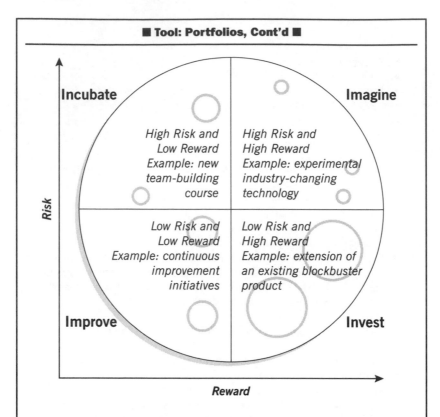

Risks and rewards for projects typically represent the Invest profile's view of value. The object of putting the creativity profiles in the background of this diagram is to illustrate that projects viewed as high risk or low reward might sometimes produce another sort of value (commonly associated with that particular profile). For example, high-risk, low-reward initiatives such as training can produce learning, valued by the Incubate profile. Larger circles (representing greater investments) usually appear in the lower-risk profiles.

Figure 4.1. Risk and Reward Diagram

- If your firm already has decision-making criteria for advancing initiatives through its portfolio process, examine these criteria and decide if they are sufficiently diverse. You can diversify your criteria by considering the following questions:
  - Have I required every project to maximize value by increasing Net Present Value, reducing cycle time, improving market impact, or reducing failure rates? Allow some of your projects to offer different kinds of value.

■ Tool: Portfolios, Cont'd ■

- Have I allowed projects to align with my strategy in different ways? Aim for diversity in alignment with strategy, strategic intent and focus, and performance measures.
- Have I balanced and diversified the type of innovations, markets, and business lines that I consider?
- Do my criteria allow a project to stretch the portfolio through radical innovation or a higher-impact initiative?
- Do my criteria allow a project to leverage the portfolio by increasing the value of products in other business lines or by effectively utilizing production platforms and programs?

Create a Continuous Stream of Ideas for an "Idea Portfolio"
- Ideas come from everywhere. The key to an idea portfolio is to seek them out and review them regularly for development opportunities. Find and document ideas from all areas of the business. Here are some useful sources of ideas:
  - Suggestion programs
  - Creativity camps (where everyone comes up with new ideas)
  - Innovation incubators (where new ventures are launched with assistance from professional service providers)
  - Listening posts (put a person to gather information in locations where new technologies are being developed)
  - Research and development scouting (understanding what is in the lab)
  - Technology foresight processes (experts and leaders try to forecast future technologies and strategically frame them—see the Forecasting tool in Chapter Three for more information on this technique)
- Put these ideas into a database so that they can be easily accessed. Target and prioritize the best ideas for development.
- Keep the flow of initiatives high so that you have plenty from which to select the best.

Launch Multiple, Diversified Types of Initiatives
- Diversify the portfolio. Different types of portfolio holdings represent different risks at different times.
- Some initiatives should be incremental in nature and aimed at improving existing business lines. Others should be breakthrough innovations that create new products, services, or markets.

Track the Progress of Initiatives Through a Tollgate Development Process
- Periodically review initiatives at distinct stages in order to monitor and adjust their progress toward value creation (see Figure 4.2). Use just a few gates or use many, depending on the level of complexity of the initiatives and the level of control that the portfolio group wants to maintain.

■ Tool: Portfolios, Cont'd ■

- Initial tollgates should focus on the merit of the initiative for its relative strategic fit with your firm's purposes, compared to other holdings in the portfolio.
- Middle gates should focus on testing the concept in limited production and markets while keeping the investment of resources as low as possible so as to reduce risk.
- Later gates should focus on the viability of the initiative as a scalable operation.
- Each gate review is an opportunity for the portfolio team to ask questions, provide advice, allocate resources, and change the initiative's management team.

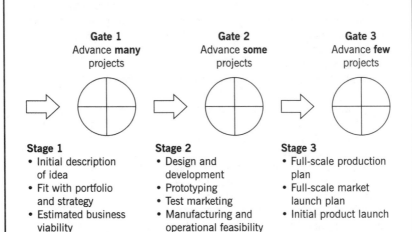

Gate 1
Advance **many**
projects

Gate 2
Advance **some**
projects

Gate 3
Advance **few**
projects

Stage 1
- Initial description of idea
- Fit with portfolio and strategy
- Estimated business viability

Stage 2
- Design and development
- Prototyping
- Test marketing
- Manufacturing and operational feasibility

Stage 3
- Full-scale production plan
- Full-scale market launch plan
- Initial product launch

Each circle represents an evaluation using the Risk and Reward Diagram. Because you want to accomplish different things at each gate, the criteria will be different. For example, early gates should have more flexible criteria and projects situated all over the diagram. Later stages should be much more selective.

Figure 4.2. The Tollgate Portfolio Review Process for Investments

■ Tool: Portfolios, Cont'd ■

- Make decisions to stop, go, modify, or hold initiatives.
- As an initiative moves from its initial phases of planning and toward institutionalization, it should become increasingly difficult for it to pass to the next gate because the resource demands will greatly increase. If too many initiatives make it to full-scale implementation, the resource base may be seriously compromised. The portfolio team needs to be tough-minded in what initiatives it allows to pass each gate.
- Be sure to learn from what you do. Try out many ideas and tolerate the failure of some of them. Have a postmortem after failed initiatives to diagnose what went wrong and derive lessons that can be applied to future projects.

Seek Synergy and Leverage
- Seek synergy from the portfolio's contents.
  - Determine potential economies of scale through multiple offerings.
  - Recognize that the value of any technology is greater if you can use it elsewhere in the portfolio, where it can help other holdings become more valuable. A seemingly unprofitable technology may become worthwhile when viewed in this light.
  - Explore the option of acquiring a product from another company to fill a hole in the portfolio.
- Leverage projects in your portfolio. That is, look for ways to use one project to help other projects in the portfolio. For example:
  - Manage products as a cluster to leverage them *as a cluster.* Sell some products or services at a loss if it will help generate business in a high-margin area.
  - Use an extension of an existing product to increase the sales of a more experimental one (say, by bundling them together to improve customer awareness).
  - Use a product to move into new technologies or markets so that other items in the portfolio will benefit.

Source: From *Creativity at Work* by Jeff DeGraff and Katherine A. Lawrence. Copyright © 2002 by John Wiley & Sons.

CHAPTER SUMMARY

The Invest profile is focused on using discipline to produce financial value with reduced risk. The practices are best suited for situations that need convergent ideas to meet an external challenge or opportunity. Through partnering and portfolios, companies in this profile hope to achieve speed and profits.

Partnering is a *mutually beneficial alliance between two or more parties* looking for opportunities to create synergy with others outside the boundaries of their unit or firm. Good partnerships offer a faster way to reach new markets or produce bundles of goods, but they do not prevent competitors from doing the same thing. In addition to speed, partnerships can improve knowledge or brand allegiance. Partnering is creative by allowing companies to produce something new that they could not have produced individually.

Portfolios are collections of products and services that are viewed as investments. Portfolios might include entire companies, individual products and services, or projects. At its best, a portfolio spreads risk across the set of holdings by using a diverse set of criteria to rigorously select and evaluate each investment throughout its development. Portfolios are creative when they are treated as an art; beyond quantitative criteria, portfolios should leverage expertise, learning, and judgment so that the individual holdings can help each other, making the whole greater than the sum of its parts.

The practices in the Invest profile put resources with good ideas, create new opportunities, and solve problems. By blending resources—whether external or internal—they leverage a company's offerings to make them worth more collectively than they are individually.

Improve Practices

Incremental Creativity Through Modular Design and Development and Process Improvement Systems

The Improve profile is about incremental creativity—modifying something that already exists to make it better. Incremental creativity practices commonly involve internally focused systems that produce a convergent solution. The risk in this situation is technical failure or not using resources effectively. The rewards are quality and optimization.

Quite often, science and engineering are at the root of the products and services in the Improve profile. These products and services involve complex systems with many interdependent parts and people; therefore, coordination within the firm requires control through a system of standardized structures and processes. Although tight control and standardization may seem to run counter to the traditional notions of creativity, it is the boundaries of the control system that make incremental creativity possible. Limiting the scope of modifications within a complex system makes change less risky and intimidating. Within the defined margins, people's minds are free to be creative. You will see this dynamic at work in the two practices we discuss in this chapter, modular design and development as a path to quality and process improvement systems as a way to optimization.

Capsule Overview:
Modular Design and Development

What modular design and development is . . .
Breaking down complex systems into parts that
can be developed and tested independently.

Because the practice of modular design and development
solves complex engineering challenges in multiple parts of a
project at the same time, products can be developed faster and
more flexibly. By keeping the connections between the pieces
consistent, employees can be creative in experimenting and testing numerous ideas within each module to find the best design.

What modular design and development gets you . . .
Flexibility within complexity.

Modular design and development is excellent for those
who desire secondary, incremental innovation, essentially building off existing science, technologies, or systems. Such situations
can be complex, and testing early and often is essential to eliminate bugs on individual pieces before they are integrated. With
this technique, numerous variations can be tested to find the optimal design with the least risk. Moreover, by allowing simulta-
neous engineering, modularity can reduce development time
and often costs as well. Modularity also permits customization
of products to meet market needs.

What modular design and development doesn't get you . . .
Discontinuous innovation.

Although modular design and development can produce
remarkable discoveries and inventions, these advances usually

represent improvements on existing products rather than a complete break with the past. Also, the inherent focus on small details often prevents anticipation of larger events or changes on the horizon. Finally, sometimes products or systems are too interrelated to lend themselves to being broken into modules.

> *When modular design and development works best . . .*
> On products or processes that are highly complex and
> contain identifiable subsystems.

Modules are useful when the complexity of developing the product or process is so great that a single team cannot manage it. Individual teams can develop their expertise in one component, concerning themselves with the design of the component and its interfaces with other parts.

■ Fitting the Pieces Together: Modularity and Modeling

Modules are independently designed units that work within a larger, integrated system or whole. Often called a *platform*, this set of subsystems and the interfaces between them compose the basic architecture on which multiple products can be based. However, modularization can only work effectively when you have deep knowledge of all the factors that influence the product design.[1]

Using platforms increases the speed and flexibility of product development by allowing modules to be swapped in and out without the cumbersome negotiations typical of complex, integrated systems. Within platforms, modules can boost the rate of innovation and change by giving engineers freedom to experiment with product design within the restrictions set by interface standards. Using modules can also enable companies to work in new ways with outside suppliers or partners. For example, the computer industry blossomed when IBM set the open standard for the subcomponents of its computer system. Manufacturers could refine and improve the subcomponents, allowing them to compete in their chosen niche markets as long as their interfaces remained faithful to the specifications.

The related technique of modeling is a second significant factor in complex design tasks. Two main kinds of modeling are common in science and engineering. Traditionally, engineers have used physical models as prototypes that approximate the behavior of the final design and allow them to test whether the components will work as expected in the real world. More recently, mathematical modeling has been used in computer simulations. The simulator acts as a virtual reality environment that permits the designers to evaluate the interactions and behaviors of the combined design models.

Early simulations and prototyping can be critical, because decisions that affect about 85 percent of the ultimate total cost of a project are typically made during the first 15 percent of a project schedule. Modeling provides "a structure, discipline, and approach that significantly enhance the rate of learning and integration in development projects."[2] In short, engineers use models because they want to "fail often in order to succeed sooner."[3]

As you will see, the tight structure of modularity and the testing benefits afforded by modeling create a rigorous structure within which creativity can happen. Within modules, product developers have the freedom to innovate and inexpensively test new ideas, producing quality components cheaper and faster.

Case Study: Taking a Legacy to the Extreme

In 1998, Bob Nero, the new CEO of Interface Systems, Inc., knew that his company had to do something different in order to survive.[4] For nearly thirty years, Interface had built a reputation for its ability to convert data from ancient mainframe legacy systems into a format that could be printed by PC-compatible printers. Although Interface was a leader in the industry, particularly for the fidelity of its output, it needed to pursue new markets. Its stock price had dropped from a high of $20 to $2 per share.

Nero saw an opening for growth into the Internet market space, but Interface needed to make the transition with the same quality that had sustained its reputation. Moreover, Nero needed his R&D team to have the speed, productivity, energy, enthusiasm, and creativity necessary to compete with other on-line businesses. In short, Interface needed to behave like a start-up, with the sustainability and quality associated with a mature company.

Nero promoted Rich Sheridan, a manager of one of the product teams, to vice president of R&D and assigned him the task of solving this problem. He also warned Sheridan that the team should be able to double in size when the company's new image began to take root.

For nearly a year, Sheridan researched his options. While learning about object-oriented programming, Sheridan found his solution: Extreme Programming. *XP,* as it is known to programmers, is a software development approach that takes programming to an "extreme" level by integrating best practices into a single system that routinized them as part of everyday work.[5] What appealed to Sheridan was that XP reduced the risk and accommodated the changes inherent in software projects by using iterative, incremental development plans, simple designs, plenty of communication and feedback, and an aggressive approach to problem solving. Moreover, XP advocated using pairs of programmers, each working together at a single computer and keyboard in a room of programming pairs working on the same project. Sheridan believed that the value system of XP could revitalize Interface and allow the company to expand its development efforts while preserving quality.

In mid-1999, Sheridan began to build what he called the "Java Factory." He switched his programmers to using Java because it was an object-oriented language that allowed modularity in the design of software applications, and it was simple to learn. After an initial trial with one XP pair, he found the results compelling. In September, he started seven XP pairs in a former manufacturing space with no walls, cement floors, large folding tables, and rolling chairs.

This is how the factory worked. The "customer" assigned to the team (in this case, one or more marketing people who knew what the products entailed) wrote up "stories" on large index cards, itemizing each of the features they wanted the final products to have. Every two weeks, Sheridan reassigned team members to new pairings, so that they were regularly cross-pollinating knowledge. The new pairs spent a couple of hours estimating how long each story would take to program—whether a day, half a week, a week, two weeks, three weeks, or four weeks. The marketing team then prioritized the entire set of story cards and scheduled the stories based on the manpower available for each upcoming two-week cycle. Finally, Sheridan assigned stories to pairs, matching stories to meet developer interests or to grow skills within the team. The assigned stories were posted on the wall for everyone to see, and their current status was color-coded so that the programmers and Sheridan could know at a glance if a pair was running behind or ahead of schedule. In addition, the overall structural metaphor of the project was displayed on the wall so that everyone could see how their part fit within the whole.

A pair began working on a story by writing a "unit test" that would allow them to find out automatically if their function worked after they had programmed it. The test was added to the existing collection of tests for the project to ensure that every incremental change of the software complied with all the previous tests. The pair then began writing the code for the story itself. While one person typed, the other one kept an eye out for potential errors and considered the big picture for their part of the project. Together they discussed what they were doing and generated ideas for solving coding challenges. If both were stuck, they could readily enlist another programmer for a quick meeting, rolling their chairs from one computer to another or to a whiteboard as they collaborated.

Several times a day, the pair integrated the new code with the old and tested it to make sure it didn't fail any tests or interfere with other programmers' code. If a unit test failed when someone added a module, the pair—and sometimes the entire group—focused on fixing it. At the end of each two-week iteration, each pair presented what they had completed, regardless of its state, to the entire company, in order to get additional feedback from their colleagues.

The programmers loved this new way of working, and they were able to produce reliable code at a good pace. At the start of February 2000, Nero said it was time for Sheridan to scale up his team. Between February and June, twenty new programmers were hired. Each one was immediately plugged into a pair so that each newcomer was productive and integrated as part of the project immediately.

The Java Factory became an enormous success. Interface had produced a group of programmers who were fluent in using a structured, modular system to quickly create reliable new software. The business results were dramatic: in 1999, Interface had the fastest-rising stock of any Michigan-based company, growing nearly 700 percent (in part due to the Internet stock boom). The following September, the company was sold to another technology firm for $17 per share.

■ Discussion: A New Interface for Programmers

Traditional design methods can result in numerous errors that propagate through the design, along with endless negotiations between engineers. In a highly complex system, even a few errors can cause catastrophic results. By employing modularity and modeling, Interface not only avoided these problems but allowed the programmers' creativity to flourish. The company's success was aided by the use of XP, which focuses on "values that serve both human and commercial needs: communication, simplicity, feedback, and courage."[6] However, the wisdom of its practices can be explained by more general concepts: modular design, iterative testing, and continual integration of the project and team.

Modular design. Modularity and the integration of modules were at the heart of the Java Factory's development system. Both the Java programming language and the project design were modular, as was the shuffling of pairs within the programming team. The stories that the programmers used made the design process more predictable, manageable, and clear, yet at the same time they gave the programmers the freedom to be creative within their individual parts. All the programmers knew how their pieces fit into the entire design because they had reviewed each story when making the time estimates, and they had worked on many parts. They aimed for simplicity in design and programming, which meant that each module was streamlined for future revisions by anyone on the team—another opportunity for creativity. Likewise, programmers became interchangeable so that Sheridan could still have productive pairs when employees were absent or new hires joined the production team.

Iterative testing. Although testing as a way of achieving quality is common practice, Interface's form of rapid prototyping has been relatively less common in the software industry. Many developers wait to do quality assurance (QA) at the end of a long development cycle. The testers are a separate group from the programmers, and their challenge is to find any bugs that the programmers missed. Meanwhile, during the QA process, the programmers cannot make progress on the program.

In contrast, by designing independent, automatic tests *before* they begin programming, XP programmers get rapid feedback on their efforts. If they have a problem, they have lost no more than a day's worth of work. Moreover, they can experiment with different approaches to a single task and know immediately whether or not it will work as desired. Creativity and quality monitoring are integral parts of the process.

Iterative testing has benefits beyond the programming domain. Customers have greater confidence in a product's quality when they can see the progress of the project and the outcomes of the tests. In fact, customers (whether internal or external) are expected to have their own "acceptance tests" that verify that the software is producing the expected results. Just as the story cards document the functionality of the program, the tests document that the program works. Because this process does not require scheduling of QA time, customers can see a tangible product faster than they otherwise would and can know exactly how far the project has progressed.

Continual integration of project and team. A key ingredient in Interface's product development approach is the way it continuously integrated the programmers' efforts. Integration solves several common problems of the product development process.

One of the disadvantages of modularity can be that product developers lose the opportunity for synergy between interdependent components in favor of the predictability and manageability of developing modules independently.[7] Also, a rapidly changing marketplace may require respecification of the product design, with implications for the modular structure of the product.[8] By continually integrating their product so that they had the most up-to-date version every night and a complete skeleton of the product (whether bare bones or fleshed out) every two weeks, Interface's programmers could easily make shifts in the product specifications at the start of any programming cycle. Further, the boundaries between modules could be redefined as needed as part of this integration process. Neither the modular structure nor the product concept were frozen for more than the length of an iteration cycle.

Integration was evident in Interface's team process as well. The layout and operations of the work space fostered communication and social networks. All facets of the project were displayed on the walls, and Sheridan found that he could manage more people than he had in the past because he no longer had to check in with each programmer to get a status report. Likewise, programmers knew where their tasks fit into the product, and how others might be affected by their programming and design decisions. Because pairs changed every two weeks, programmers gained exposure to other parts of the project and to each other's capabilities. Switching pairs also provided new hires with mentoring and a resource for general questions. All programmers were within earshot of each other so that an expert could help another pair when necessary, yet experts were not confined to working only on what they were good at doing. In a pair and as part of the larger team, each programmer felt committed to observing coding standards, a shared design, and regular testing—practices uncommon in the typical "renegade cowboy" model of programming.

The surprising efficiencies of working in pairs. One of the first criticisms of XP programming pairs is "Why would you want to double your programming hours?" Pair programming at Interface was actually more efficient in many ways. Just as pilots or surgeons work together, the programmers could have one person program while the other person was tracking the larger issues, finding resources in a manual, or just making sure they were not making any mistakes. They felt more responsible for using unit tests and observing standards when they were working together because they kept each other accountable.[9] Overall, less time was spent generating, finding, and repairing errors compared to the individual programmer mode of work. Rarely would a pair sit at an absolute standstill as they tried to solve a problem, because they had an ongoing dialogue with each other and access to the other pairs in the room. Since then, Sheridan has applied the "pair" practice to other domains, realizing that adding resources sometimes *increases* efficiency.

The pairs also were more confident about delving into the unknown. Previously Sheridan found that when solo programmers were asked to try a new kind of task, they would ask to take a course first, so there were delays while the person scheduled and attended the training. Instead, his pairs were eager to charge ahead with just a manual in hand because they knew they could explore it together, making the task considerably less overwhelming. Like two travelers heading for someplace unknown, one would drive while the other would navigate.

Ultimately, the XP system at Interface provided substantial structure but also tremendous creative flexibility. Programmers were able to be creative through designing tests, experimentation, and translating a "story" into simple, elegant code. Their creativity produced the quality that Interface needed, and the programmers' pleasure in their work created the sustainable energy and enthusiasm that Nero and Sheridan needed.

■ **Using Modular Design and Development:**
Creativity Within Known Boundaries

In essence, modular design and development offers a highly
flexible, low-risk path to successful, high-quality outcomes.
Modularity allows engineers, scientists, and designers to play
within the boundaries of a complex system. Modeling, whether
prototyping or simulation, helps to increase "planned" errors in
a rapid, cost-effective way—in contrast to late-stage, unplanned
errors that are expensive and inconvenient.

Technology and tight standards enable both modularity and
modeling. At its most basic, a platform can serve as the foundation for several products that swap parts in and out. However, a
particular platform can be extended to become the basis for another, completely different product. For example, the functionally restrictive standard for cell phones, called GSM, also enables
PDAs and other handheld devices. In fact, sometimes the redesign of a platform is more valuable than the product it facil-
itates. Called architectural innovation, the reorganization of
platform components and their links can substantially alter the
nature of an entire industry, as these subtle redesigns can displace
the market dominators.[10] For example, new entrants overtook the
manufacture of photolithographic machines for making semi-
conductors four times over two decades. Each time the newcomers invented a way to shift a part of the machinery in a way
that dramatically improved throughput without altering the
basic manufacturing process.[11] Likewise, incremental radicalism,
changing only one component of a platform to incorporate a
"radical" technology, can redefine the performance and value of
an old technology, as when Xerox dramatically improves the performance of its copiers and printers by swapping in a new type
of laser.[12] Thinking about platforms this way can open further opportunities for creativity and invention.

Indeed, modular design and development isn't just relevant to software and computing. Boeing designed and developed its 777 jet using a computer system that helped track conflicts between independently designed components during the development process.[13] Similarly, pharmaceutical companies develop new drugs by testing various agents separately, and as they achieve success, they recombine them into larger compounds. Ultimately, they build these compounds into commercially available drugs by adding new chemical agents to the basic foundations. Even newspapers and news services can be considered modular, as fully developed stories are provided by local reporters and external news suppliers and edited to fit the space available. Such processes allow both quality and quick assembly. Of course, the more complex the project, the more difficult the process of chunking the system into modules and defining the interfaces. Moreover, routine integration is less frequent in a more complex system.

Functionally restrictive or technical systems can seem so mechanistic and controlling that typically "creative" people, such as those found in the Imagine profile, may be turned off by them.[14] Yet such systems do allow substantial creativity. The standards provide a base "language" that saves developers the trouble of reinventing a form of notation. Like musicians who compose within the limits of a musical notation system and a particular instrument, the product developers are free to focus their creative energies on invention within the boundaries of the structure.

■ Tool: Modular Design and Development ■

Desired Outcomes
- Methodically develop products and services with reduced risk.
- Devise clear methods for designing quality.
- Adapt and customize products or services to keep up with a changing marketplace.
- Reduce wasted effort by avoiding reactive behaviors.

Time Needed
- Sessions: Half a day to one day in every iteration.
- Frequency: At the beginning of each iteration.

Overview
- This tool can have many benefits, but some aspects are better suited for certain types of projects. These exceptions are noted throughout this description.
- This is an iterative, ongoing process that should allow you to shape your product over time. Decide the length of your iteration cycle at the start of the project. This span of time should be no longer than you can comfortably allow your project to be on the "wrong" track. In other words, if you were to identify an important product change, what is the longest you could wait to incorporate a new feature into the development process? How much existing work would you be willing to throw away? Based on your available manpower, this cycle length will also determine the amount of the project you can accomplish in any given cycle.

Setting
- A location in the company where products and services are developed or produced. Co-locate the development team if possible to improve communication and foster team spirit.

Materials
- Index cards, sticky notes, or other visual diagramming systems. White boards and bulletin boards should be in a common area, ideally visible to all.

Who Should Participate
- Operating managers, product and service developers, technicians, manufacturers, marketing experts (including internal or external constituencies to whom you are delivering the product).
- The size of your firm and the size of your project will determine whether certain aspects of this modular design and development tool will be feasible. For example:

■ Tool: Modular Design and Development, Cont'd ■

- If your firm is so small that only a few people can perform a certain en-gineering task, then you will be unable to use rotating assignments. A set of four to six individuals with comparable skills is the lower limit.
- If your project or firm is very large, it is best to break the project into larger components and then subdivide these components as described here. Aim for no more than forty developers in one collaborative group. For example, an engine is a defined component of an airplane or vehicle, yet it can be developed in smaller modules.

Facilitation
- Often the manager of a development team or the chief design engineer plays this role.

Steps in the Process

Define the Current Specifications of the Product
- Identify generally, then specifically, what your product will do.
- Have customers or sales experts break the product down into identifiable features or components that end users will perceive and value. Be as specific as possible to help deconstruct the product into the smallest possible pieces. List these features or components on individual index cards so that they can be posted or circulated.
- Include people with expertise in understanding the relationship between various technologies. (For example, a cell phone has numerous internal components that are invisible to the end user.)
- Prioritize the features by what is essential or most important. In doing this, consider what the end users will value the most. You may end up eliminating some features or putting them on hold.
- The greater the complexity, the more up-front structure you'll need to create, and the less allowance you have for change. In such situa-tions, you will also need to group interdependent parts that cannot be separated.

Create Standards for Development
- Create an image, diagram, or metaphor that explains how the entire project fits together. This should be intelligible to all involved.
- If components of the product are independent but have inputs or outputs that relate to other components, define the interface between them (the data, connectors, geometries, materials specifications, and so on).
- If multiple people or teams will work with the same component at differ-ent times (especially in software development), be sure to define conven-tions or other language and notation standards.

□

■ Tool: Modular Design and Development, Cont'd ■

Estimate and Assign Time and Resources
- Gather the group of engineers and technicians who will develop the product. Have each individual review and estimate the time and materials necessary to design and test each component on which they might work. The time estimates can be fairly general, but should range from a day to twice the length of your iteration cycle.
- If necessary, divide components into even smaller pieces. Make sure you note dependencies between components and constraints imposed by adjacent parts of the system.
- Once each component has an estimate from every person, assign that component a general estimate that represents the estimate given by the majority of the estimators.
- In a design that has many optional features, give the estimations to the customers or sales experts who defined the project scope. Ask them to select the components that are their greatest priority for the upcoming iteration of development. They can select only as many components as can be completed by your available developers. Otherwise, decide what components must be implemented first from a perspective of design needs.
- Assign the components to developer pairs or teams. Assign one or more components per iteration to a set of developers based on the estimates given by those people. If a large module has been subdivided into independent parts, you might assign two or three people from a larger team to work on each part. Remember that a set of developers should receive no more work than the iteration length allows!

Simulate, Model, or Prototype
- During each iteration, post what components have been assigned to each set of developers. If your group is geographically distributed, this might be an on-line monitoring system, but if the developers are co-located, a physical representation is preferable.
- As developers begin, complete, or set aside each component, they should indicate this so that all developers know the status of the modules and of the project in general.
- Before building the first prototype, each team should determine how the component will be tested and what would be a successful outcome. Test each component as it is completed.
- Regularly (as appropriate, for example, every day or every week), components should be integrated and tested as a larger unit, particularly if they depend on each other. As multiple components are integrated, look for ways that their interfaces might be improved.

■ Tool: Modular Design and Development, Cont'd ■

- If the product is large or testing is expensive or time-consuming, simulations might suffice as an alternative to physical prototypes.

Identify and Communicate Lessons Learned
- At the end of an iteration, gather the entire group assigned to the project as well as other stakeholders and review progress. Identify any components that are still under development and any tests that have failed.
- Identify any useful ways in which you have solved particular challenges or integrated multiple components. Encourage participants to share these solutions with the other developers so that these processes can be replicated elsewhere or in a later project.

Begin the Next Iteration
- Return to the first step of this process in which you identify the components needed. At the start of an iteration is the time to add, drop, or reprioritize components. If some components appear to be more difficult or less worthwhile than initially expected, take these shifts into account.
- Reestimate the amount of time to produce each component, including those that have development time remaining, because estimates may shift on the basis of lessons learned.
- Assign new components to new sets of developers. You can maximize the cross-pollination of experience and specific knowledge by redistributing pair or team members and assigning them to new tasks. This also encourages collective ownership of the final product and avoids the development of knowledge silos.

Source: From *Creativity at Work* by Jeff DeGraff and Katherine A. Lawrence. Copyright © 2002 by John Wiley & Sons.

Capsule Overview:
Process Improvement Systems

What process improvement systems are . . .
A method for designing the organizational structure and
its systems to enable incremental enhancements.

Process improvement systems emphasize the "craft" of production. Groups using process improvement systems begin by analyzing data that suggest what is working optimally and what could be better. The groups then dismantle their problems to develop an array of small wins, codified as roles and procedures.

What process improvement systems get you . . .
A controlled, low-risk system.

The emphasis of process improvement systems is to have optimized, responsive, and lower-risk systems in place. Optimization is the effective utilization of available resources such as manpower, knowledge, time, physical materials and supplies, manufacturing capacity, and capital. By optimizing, organizations can do more with less, and design and manufacturing follows a known path to success. Creativity happens within the boundaries defined for the roles and procedures.

What process improvement systems don't get you . . .
Radical change or opportunity.

The carefulness of optimization means that nothing big or unexpected happens. Consequently, process improvement systems do not create radical innovation, big change, or new markets. Moreover, the systems are so precise and risk averse that the firm does not encourage learning through the failure cycle.

When process improvement systems work best . . .
Your firm needs to reliably deliver large
volumes of products or services.

Process improvement systems are excellent whenever you need to make, sell, or support anything in large volumes. They are also ideal when failure is not an option, as when there is a right way and a wrong way to do something. Typically, clear roles and structures are emphasized when the process is large and complex.

Case Study: A Clear System for Creativity

Toyota founder Kiichiro Toyoda was committed to research and development.[15] World War II had devastated Japan, but the ensuing occupation brought some unexpected benefits. During the Korean War, Japan was used as a manufacturing and logistics hub. Well-educated former Japanese military leaders were encouraged to run key industries and were taught the latest "scientific" processes. These processes developed into systems now known as total quality management, continuous improvement, just-in-time inventory, and lean manufacturing. Quickly, Japanese manufacturing techniques developed to be on a par with those in the West. In the postwar environment of the 1950s, Toyota launched the innovative four-wheel-drive Land Cruiser, the full-size Crown, and the small-size Corona. Suddenly, a Japanese company was making quality cars for a rapidly growing Asian market.

In 1973, the competitive landscape changed with the OPEC oil embargo, which sent Americans and Europeans scampering for fuel-efficient automobiles. General Motors, Ford, and Chrysler had yet to develop cars for this market, which allowed Toyota to raise its presence from an insignificant market share to leadership in the sale of small and mid-size sedans. Perched at the top of every quality rating from JD Powers to *Consumer Reports*, Toyota took its most audacious step in 1989 with the launch of a luxury brand, Lexus. Besides challenging the brand dominance of European elites like Mercedes and BMW, Lexus produced advanced technologies that appeared in Toyota products of subsequent years and helped to protect its core markets. By the year 2000, Toyota appeared near the top of every list: Fortune 500, Most Admired Firms, and Best-Known Brands. Toyota had become synonymous with fabulous manufacturing practices.

To accomplish this, Toyota's leaders looked for opportunities to create a structure that would systematically reduce wasted resources and time while integrating newer technology into existing products. For them, organizational design was like putting a puzzle together. They were always looking for a more efficient way to buy parts, sell cars, and serve customers—and their performance in these areas eventually became legendary. Today, there is little radical innovation in Toyota's approach because of the complexity of manufacturing and distribution and the large capital investments necessary for the auto industry. Instead, creativity is incremental in order to lower risk. This depends on a highly skilled and flexible workforce and the integration of roles and responsibilities.

Authority is clearly defined at all levels. Technically astute functional supervisors are expected to mentor, train, and develop their junior engineers. The actual work of each junior engineer is routinely monitored and evaluated at each step of the project. Moreover, engineers are trained to perform all the standard work in a particular specialty so that they can be locally rotated to different projects. The rotation system ensures that competencies are retained and passed along to new "generations" working in that functional area. At higher levels, an engineer might rotate out of a product or functional area to develop a complementary expertise and to promote a broader view of design needs.

In contrast to the practice of typical American and European firms, where the brand manager makes many of the design decisions, at Toyota the chief engineer is also the lead designer for the development of a new vehicle. This person maintains understanding of the big picture to guarantee that the car is successfully integrated. Combined with the highly developed expertise of functional engineers, knowledge and experience of both the current vehicle and previous projects is retained.

Information transfer at Toyota is extremely efficient. Within each department or location, simple checklists of work plans and procedures are derived from previous projects so that the knowledge and learning is preserved in the organization for use on each new project. These checklists are maintained by the people doing the work, so that the checklists are kept in alignment with the current best practices. These checklists are succinct, relevant, and therefore actually used. Likewise, verbal communication is constant and focused on solving one problem at a time. All the engineers know their own parts and how they fit into the greater system.

In 1997, Toyota introduced the Prius, the first mass-market hybrid electric-and-gas-powered car. In 2000, it launched a series of exciting new vehicles and updates aimed at attracting younger customers. At the same time, the company built a powerful on-line network for buying, financing, and servicing vehicles. Anticipating the unprecedented growth driven by the emergence of China as a viable market, Toyota reached an agreement with the Chinese government to produce passenger cars for the single largest market in the world.

Curiously, Toyota's extensive controls and clear systems support its ability to invent. Toyota's brand of creativity may be incremental, but over time, it adds up, making the firm an industry leader admired across the globe.

■ Discussion: Toyota's Formula for Institutionalized Creativity

At first glance, Toyota may not appear to be a very creative firm. There is little tolerance for the "do your own thing" or "express yourself" style of American individualism. Because cars are complex and take a long time to develop, Toyota views radical change as extremely risky. Instead, creativity must be incremental and methodical, drawing on a foundation of engineering expertise. To manufacture high-quality automobiles efficiently, Toyota needs to instill creativity as an essential part of everyday work—just part of the job.

Toyota institutionalizes creativity safely and methodically in two basic ways. First, a clear hierarchy standardizes roles and responsibilities. Second, simple rules and standards serve in place of elaborate processes.

□

Clear hierarchy. In Toyota's organization, everyone has a clearly defined role. Coordination happens through social norms and standards. Specifically, the product development hierarchy is supervised by a chief engineer with long tenure and experience, and senior engineers monitor each functional area. These supervisors pass down knowledge and expertise, both technical and managerial. Their role is to make sure that information gathered from prior research and testing is not lost to new generations of auto designs. As in the old guilds of Europe, in which master craftsmen passed on their knowledge to younger apprentices, Toyota passes on the craft of product design and development through its organizational structure.

Younger engineers are expected to know their roles and understand their relationship with other parts of the organization or their subsystem, while more senior engineers are rotated to other departments. Senior engineers' interaction with others keeps knowledge flowing and them from becoming local repositories of knowledge that might be lost in the future or unavailable to other parts of the organization. Rotation also introduces new ideas and a fresh perspective to old approaches that might otherwise become stale or hidebound under the guidance of an old-timer.[16] At the same time, chief engineers make sure new ideas do not disregard information that is important to the product. Together, these role structures enable engineers to be creative within the systems necessary for creating efficiently.

Simple rules and standards. Toyota's structure includes simple rules and standards maintained by departments. Although rules and roles seem rigid and unlikely to produce great ideas, structures actually open opportunities to be creative within the boundaries that are set.[17] People are not paralyzed by an infinite number of possibilities for improving the organization, its systems, or its products. Instead, they are encouraged from the start to contribute small, concrete suggestions. They are highly motivated to contribute in this way because Japanese suggestion systems traditionally encourage group collaboration to solve a problem, along with recognition and feedback for solutions that are implemented. In fact, at Japanese companies, including Toyota, employees identify and implement more than forty suggestions per person per year![18]

Moreover, simple guidelines that support the organization's mission help teams move swiftly and surely. Essentially, creativity doesn't only happen when inventing a new product. Rather, creativity can and should happen throughout the entire process of making and distributing that product. A fine painting displays the art of concept or composition, but the craft of using the paint or capturing perspective is also essential to the final result. The craft of making new cars at Toyota is partly accomplished by simplifying measures to their essence. Such a system of simple measures (such as staffing levels or number of unique product parts) helps employees track truly valuable improvements for the company. Creativity at Toyota fits within acceptable boundaries of the firm. Individuals offer their bright ideas as contributing members of the organization, and simple, clear structures encourage creativity without causing interference in the larger system. In this way, creativity allows the firm to do the most with its resources.

■ Using Process Improvement Systems: Achieving Optimization Through Common Standards

When the nature of work or the laws of nature impose restrictions—and the consequences of failure are severe—rigor is essential. One way of optimizing under these conditions is to apply structures and standards that encourage creativity within the margins.

The best approach for most organizations that have to optimize in a constrained environment is to establish a few concrete, simple rules—ideally two to seven of them—that are tailored to a single process. These rules should be specific and sensible enough to give guidance, not so general that their opposite might be true and not so vague that employees cannot tell when they have been met. For example, at the hearing-aid manufacturer Oticon, any project that loses a key member is stopped.[19] The simple rule allows no doubt of the consequences. When the situation that prompted a simple rule has changed, be sure the rules are brought up-to-date.[20] Toyota's simple rules and checklists are living documents that reflect current understanding of the company's capabilities.[21] The frequency of your own updates depends on the volatility of your industry. For example, financial institutions meet several times a day to recalibrate rules that pertain to buying, selling, and holding investments. With effective rules, employees know their direction and purpose at all times.

In a sense, the situations faced by complex organizations trying to optimize are much like the task of building a cathedral during the Middle Ages. The architects and craftsmen had physical, material, religious, and symbolic constraints: Gravity dictated how arches and domes could be built. The common supplies were stone, wood, and glass. The Catholic Church had guidelines for the floor plan and dictated much of the allowable symbolism of the day. Yet over many years of construction, numerous specialized craftsmen collaborated within those guidelines and constraints, and together they produced beautiful architecture and works of art that have lasted for centuries. Today we appreciate their immense creativity—creativity that flourished within the clear, established framework of roles and rules.

The process improvement systems tool will help you to analyze and reorganize the roles and rules that apply to a process or problem at your work place. You can use this tool on a regular basis to create a system for ongoing, optimizing improvements.

■ Tool: Process Improvement Systems ■

Desired Outcomes
- Optimize resource use.
- Manage complex activities effectively.
- Align organizational design with key processes.
- Establish and articulate clear roles and responsibilities.

Time Needed
- Planning and setup: Allow sufficient time to gather supporting materials.
- Sessions: Variable. Allow two or three hours when you first begin using this tool, as people will need time to grow comfortable with it. The session length will also depend on the magnitude of the problems.
- Frequency: Daily, weekly, or at least every two or three months. Consider the urgency of the problems.

Setting
- A quiet meeting place, without interruptions.

Materials
- Information on problems and improvement opportunities, key processes, organizational roles and responsibilities, performance metrics, and program plans.

Who Should Participate
- A cross-functional group of people who have an interest in improving a process or solving a problem that they know and understand.

Facilitation
- Anyone familiar with the group and its problem and who has effective facilitation skills.

Steps in the Process

Discuss the Issue and Opportunities for Improvement
- Assemble a cross-functional group from multiple areas and levels of your organization that have a direct relationship with the problem. For example, if you are having a problem with marketing a new product such as a refrigerator because it has a higher-than-average repair rate, you might invite members from your marketing, product design, and manufacturing operations to attend this gathering. Some of these people should have the knowledge to contribute toward a solution, while others must be in a position to make decisions that can transform ideas into action. Essentially, these people should be experts in their area, and you want them to be creative within their area of technical competence.[22]
- Start by introducing the problem in a clear and concise statement. Ask the group to help improve the statement of the problem. Often the clarification of the problem goes halfway to solving it.

■ Tool: Process Improvement Systems, Cont'd ■

- Ask the group, "What does this problem stop us from doing?" That is, Why is this a problem? The idea here is to identify a clear intended outcome. The group should identify what is to be gained by coming up with a solution. If there is little to gain, or the problem may have hidden advantages, it may not be worth the time to solve it.
- Next, have the group speculate what could be causing the problem. List the possibilities on sticky notes and post them on the wall. Cluster these underlying causes into categories, such as manufacturing or engineering. Identify which cluster is the most likely root cause of the problem. From these sticky notes, restate these root causes as the problem. Ask the group, "If we solve this underlying problem are we likely to solve, at least in part, the original problem statement?" If the answer is "yes," proceed to the next step. If the answer is "no," revisit your clusters and reshape them into an improved underlying problem that can pass this test.
- The underlying cause of the problem is now the problem statement.

State the Facts of the Case
- Now that you have identified what the problem is and why it is a problem, ask the group what they know about:
  - How does it occur?
  - Where does it occur?
  - When does it occur?
  - Whose problem is it?
- On a flip chart, detail what you know about the problem and what you would like to know about the problem. Make a list of information to be gathered on the problem and who might be able to get this data.
- At this point the dimensions of the problem should be relatively clear.

Select Opportunities for Improvement
- First, have the group identify opportunities for improving the problem. This can include anything such as stopping or starting a new activity or moving responsibility from one person to another. This is a chance to be creative and propose suggestions that involve any of the relevant functional areas. Put these responses on sticky notes.
- Cluster the ideas by type of solution, and prioritize them by feasibility.
- From these potential solutions, identify some small and quick wins and assign them to subgroups or other groups throughout the organization. Each assignment should have a goal and a deliverable date, and conditions, such as budgetary or quality constraints if necessary. The key is to let these small groups solve their part of the problem as they see fit. Allow enough time for some limited experimentation.

Review and Revise
- After two or three weeks, reconvene the meeting to review what's working and what's not. This step can be repeated indefinitely if necessary.

■ Tool: Process Improvement Systems, Cont'd ■

Members of the group can offer advice and assistance. If it appears that a subgroup is not making sufficient progress, its tasks can be modified, reassigned, or stopped altogether to pursue a more productive approach.
- The group should track the progress toward solving the problem. As small wins begin to materialize, other opportunities for improvement will emerge and the group can choose to pursue them or solve other pending problems.
- Constantly review how roles and responsibilities need to be modified to support these improvements. Consider if there is any secondary liability to changing the organizational structure. For example, if a person is taken off one job and put on another, the reassignment may create a problem somewhere else in the process.

Integrate Process Improvements
- Look for opportunities to test and integrate these small wins into the organization's processes. Don't try to implement them all at once. For example, redesign only the first stage of a process on a project that has a limited production run. Get creative in small ways. Remember, this is work in progress.
- Look for barriers you had not previously considered, such as other processes at cross-purposes. Convene problem-solving sessions to resolve specific integration problems. Collect data and audit your progress on performance benchmarks. Most important, determine if the problem solving and improvement activities have produced their intended results.

Extend What You Have Learned
- Once the improvements have shown results, convene a group to develop simple rules of thumb based on the lessons learned. For example:
    - *Technical Rules:* Best ways to perform certain tasks, tricks of the trade, and safety procedures
    - *Situational Rules:* Time allocation, priorities, and boundaries
    - *Behavioral Rules:* Actions, values, and attitudes
    - *Leadership Rules:* Leadership style, mission, and esprit de corps
    - *Financial Rules:* Expense approvals, rates of return, and budgets
- Make these rules specific, relevant, targeted, and feasible. Relate stories of when the rules worked and didn't work and why. Your rules should be revised regularly since they evolve from what is learned through these limited experiments. They translate insight into operating principles.
- Ultimately, your rules can be applied to future improvements to your structure and systems. They help you document solutions so that they can be used later. By structuring them as rules of thumb, you make them more readily accessible to future problem solvers in your area.

Source: From *Creativity at Work* by Jeff DeGraff and Katherine A. Lawrence. Copyright © 2002 by John Wiley & Sons.

CHAPTER SUMMARY

The Improve profile is focused on incremental creativity in a situation where errors are expensive, dangerous, or not tolerated. The practices in this profile are best suited for situations that need internally focused systems to produce a convergent solution. Through modular design and development and process improvement systems, companies in this profile hope to achieve quality and optimization.

Modular design and development is a means for solving complex design and engineering challenges by breaking down systems into parts that can be developed and tested independently. This process allows experimentation and customization in the design and development of modules while often reducing development time and costs. It is best for situations that need extensive testing and revision.

Process improvement systems involve designing the organizational structure and its systems to enable incremental enhancements. By dismantling and analyzing the work processes in the organization, employees can optimize the work roles and rules that guide the "craft" of production. It is particularly well suited for companies that need to make, sell, or support in large volumes.

The practices in the Improve profile allow employees to express their creativity as they work within the boundaries of the system. Although highly structured systems and standards appear to be the opposite of traditional concepts of creativity, limiting the scope of complex problems can make them less intimidating and easier to solve.

Incubate Practices

Sustainable Creativity Through Talent Scouting and Idea Spaces

T he Incubate profile is about finding and nurturing people in the best possible environment. Incubate practices turn your employees into your most valuable asset. This approach is most appropriate when the situation calls for building flexible, sustainable creativity by drawing on divergent abilities internal to the company. The rewards of the Incubate profile are community and knowledge, whereas the risk in this situation is an absence of shared values and failure to learn things useful in the long term in favor of pursuing short-term goals.

Although this kind of creativity is the most sustainable, it also can demand the most time and patience, and the rewards are not often immediately seen or realized. Because Incubate practices do not always offer a straight path to strategic goals, people who incubate creativity must trust that the investment in capable people who are motivated to develop additional creative skills will pay substantial returns in the long run. The rewards are more than just profits. Incubating creativity can create a stronger sense of community and employee satisfaction, motivation, and loyalty. Employees become more capable of tapping into their own deep knowledge and the information resources around them. You will see these dynamics at work in the two tools discussed in this chapter: talent scouting and idea spaces.

Capsule Overview: Talent Scouting

What talent scouting is . . . Selecting high-potential
people with the right attitude and basic skills and giving
them experiences to support their growth.

Each of the people you select should have the ability to
make the entire team flourish. As they spend time in the organization, they get opportunities to see and do the practices they
need for peak performance. Eventually, they will teach and mentor newcomers.

What talent scouting gets you . . .
Responsive, adaptable people.

Talent scouting develops your employees' ability to be high
performers for the long term. Moreover, they will have the ability to adapt to new situations as they arise. Rather than being
trapped within a narrow set of competencies that apply to limited circumstances, employees who are empowered to shape
their work develop the competencies that allow them to repeatedly generate and build on new ideas. They also cultivate in-
house knowledge resources that will help them accomplish their
goals. By finding and developing good people, you create a
good culture, and everybody wins.

What talent scouting doesn't get you . . .
Systematic, predictable outcomes.

This practice allows ideas to come in their own time, not in
any systematic way. Consequently, neither the pace of innovation nor the earnings generated by this approach are predictable.
Further, the projects that self-directed employees generate are

not guaranteed to align with the firm's strategic goals, especially in the short term.

When talent scouting works best . . .
You can select the employees you want.

Talent scouting is most viable when managers have some say over human resource practices. Choosing who is the most capable for the job is not a task that can be delegated. In addition, talent scouting works best when managers are encouraged to value diversity in employees so as to achieve adaptability to an uncertain future.

Case Study: Building the Best Workforce

In the early 1990s, Home Depot was opening stores all over Dade County, Florida.[1] Home Depot's practice was to staff its stores with the best people it could find and create an environment where they would feel a sense of ownership in the company. The company looked for new hires who had the experience to serve customers well—off-season general contractors, retired plumbers and electricians, and even its competitors' best employees. Upon being hired, each sales associate was assigned an eight-foot section of the store. The associates were fully responsible for keeping the shelves stocked and for assisting customers in their designated areas. The expectation was that the associates would take initiative as if they were the sole proprietors of their part of the store.

In August 1992, Hurricane Andrew tore through South Florida with apocalyptic fury. It left twenty-five people dead, 108,000 homes leveled, and $20 billion in damage. In the days that followed, the stricken community received vital support from Home Depot stores throughout South Dade. Although the company's headquarters had an emergency hurricane response plan on paper, the people working in the local stores were the ones to come through with the desperately needed know-how and materials. Maria Perez, an employee at one South Dade Home Depot, lost her own home to the hurricane. Yet she joined other colleagues in sorting through what was left of her store so that it could be reopened for customers as quickly as possible. Bruce Berg, a merchandising vice president in the southeast division, was on site to assess the damage. He determined that all prices would stay at pre-hurricane levels even though the store could have raised prices based on demand. Furthermore, certain materials used to cover up windows were to be sold at cost. Berg informed national headquarters of his decision after it had been put into effect. His mandate, which cost Home Depot millions of dollars in potential profits, was fully supported by top management. "Just do what is right now," they told him, "We'll worry about the other stuff later."[2]

Home Depot's response to the hurricane crisis was a manifestation of a code of conduct that permeates the entire company. Employees like Maria Perez so identified with the company's mission that they felt compelled to assist others in rebuilding their homes in spite of losing their own. Bruce Berg was authorized to make the on-site decision to hold prices without conferring with his superiors. As the co-founders of Home Depot, Arthur Blank and Bernie Marcus, put it, "With the right value system and the right knowledge to do their job, people can be trusted to make the right decisions."[3]

After southern Florida was back on its feet, the governor named Home Depot corporate citizen of the year. By earning customer loyalty, Home Depot came to enjoy an even stronger market position in South Florida. One example: the Cutler Ridge store, which opened its doors three days before the hurricane flattened it, was originally expected to earn $500,000 per week. After the hurricane, the store reopened to bring in $3 million per week.

■ Discussion: Choosing and Developing
the Right Talent for Sustainable Creativity

To succeed in a competitive marketplace, Home Depot believes that employees should take responsibility for their work. To that end, the stores hire capable employees and let them do what they think is best. Every aspect of management is based on this idea: employees are responsible for making decisions, implementing ideas, determining prices, selecting new employees, and providing excellent customer service. At all levels, Home Depot is decentralized, giving authority at the individual level, on the grounds that the front-line employees who have contact with customers can best decide how to allocate resources.

This approach is key to Home Depot's success. Several components fit together to make this approach work: careful hiring, diverse teams of employees, and empowerment and ownership.

Careful hiring. The Incubate profile is about building sustainable creativity by hiring high-potential people and helping them do the right thing. In contrast, many companies hire according to some set of criteria that reflect only the Invest profile. For example, an assertive, competitive person may be effective at producing short-term results, but a positive hindrance when it comes to building a cooperative culture over the long term.

Often, companies also hire according to a narrow set of criteria, matching "qualifications" to detailed job descriptions. In contrast, Home Depot's president and COO, Arthur Blank, said the company's rule of thumb is to "hire people who have a lot greater capacity than the job that they were given to do."[4] Instead of trying to hire the right person for the right job, Home Depot picks people with the attitude, skills, and experience to fit in any number of positions.

Once hired, employees receive continuous reinforcement of Home Depot's principles. Because each department does its own hiring and training, the current employees have a stake in selecting the most capable people and being role models for them. Over time, new hires learn how to succeed in the Home Depot culture. Outstanding employees are promoted to visible positions within the company so that it is clear what the organization expects and values.

Diverse teams of employees. Diverse teams are important for Incubate practices because one never knows exactly what the organization will need to solve a problem, satisfy a customer, or fill a market niche. Diversity can be expressed through ways of thinking, functional expertise, prior experience, social class, gender, and cultural, social, racial, and ethnic groups. Ironically, the one type of diversity that undermines Incubate practices is in values and attitudes, which help hold the community together.

Another useful index of diversity is how people think of themselves as contributors; these distinctions are their "signature skills."[5] Such signature skills might be what tasks they prefer, how they go about approaching a task or problem, and how they prefer to get the task done. Some experts even advocate having people work together who are completely polarized in their views. This approach, called "creative abrasion," is thought to transform the creative process by forcing coworkers to incorporate their opposing perspectives.[6] By hiring a variety of people with technical expertise in different areas, Home Depot constructs a team that is capable of helping customers and meeting their needs. Teams do not need to have every technical expertise in advance; in fact, the experience of being part of a team without every skill set is also beneficial for encouraging personal learning and development.[7] In this situation team members learn from each other, and they recognize and accept that learning is a necessary part of getting their job done.

The size of the team matters, too. Extensive research and observation of teams suggests that most teams are small by necessity, and the most effective teams have about six to twelve members. Teams that are larger than twelve or fifteen people are generally unwieldy: scheduling meeting time and space is difficult, the members are unlikely to coalesce under a shared vision, and the project is less likely to get participants' full investment.[8] The goal in formulating a team of an appropriate size is to have enough people to handle the project—particularly if the project is highly technical—yet to keep the group small enough to allow cohesion and a sense of shared purpose and energy. If you must have a larger group, consider breaking it into several subteams, which is what Home Depot does to ensure having experts in each area of the store.

Empowerment and ownership. Empowerment is a loaded term, with different connotations for different people. However, most managers describe empowerment as a system in which the employees have responsibility, authority, and accountability for making and implementing decisions according to the values and mission of the organization. Successfully implementing an empowerment approach requires that the employees are free to choose how they do their work, that they care about what they do, that they know they can do it, and that they know others will listen to them.[9]

Home Depot empowers its front-line employees by relying on them to know exactly what the customer needs. In many cases, Home Depot's associates are well informed because they have worked closely with similar customers in previous jobs. Ironically, in many companies, front-line or service people such as delivery drivers, repair technicians, and field representatives are often marginalized, but they are the people who *really* know the problems that customers face. Unfortunately, upper-level managers are more likely to pay marketing specialists to research customer needs because they expect that fancy surveys will better identify the problem.[10] Turning to one's own employees can often solve the problem more effectively and less expensively.

Successful empowerment involves hiring and developing people who are intrinsically motivated to perform well in their work. In addition, job design encourages intrinsic motivation when employees have substantial autonomy, the opportunity to deploy a variety of skills, meaningful task outcomes, and sufficient feedback to help them govern their own performance.[11]

Empowerment goes hand in hand with a sense of ownership. Ownership can be psychological and financial. Home Depot
encourages both. By assigning each associate to an eight-foot section of merchandise, the company encourages the associates to
take ownership responsibility for their part of the store. If management gave the employees a predetermined plan, they would
be likely to follow it without making their own contributions. Instead, like many Japanese firms who welcome employee ideas as
a way of improving the company's performance,[12] Home Depot
relies on employee initiative to solve problems better than top-
down mandates would. Again the key is intrinsic motivation
rather than external rewards. Home Depot does also reward employees with stock options and performance-based compensation,
but underlying this reward system is a culture that motivates with
more than pay.

With these principles, Home Depot has created a workplace
that encourages employee commitment and satisfaction, and it
welcomes customers with great service and competitive prices.
The company derives sustainable creativity by recognizing, and
acting on, the principle that people are the strength and the competitive strategy of the organization.

■ Using Talent Scouting:
Turning High Potential into High Performance

Incubate practices are well suited for the kind of organizations
that have decided that what they offer to their customers is their
people. For example, McKinsey & Co., one of the top consulting
firms in the world, is known for hiring the smartest graduates it
can find and teaching them how to consult. The finest educational organizations do this, too. What any Ivy League or top-
tier university does is gather together bright people who thrive
through association with each other. In such a context, what

holds people together and points them in the same direction is shared values.

In fact, most successful firms that use tools like talent scouting follow a similar approach: hiring for a good attitude and sufficient skill and experience, empowering employees to take risks and learn from their mistakes, and keeping them together through shared values. Ritz-Carlton, for example, is known for letting any employee spend up to $2,000—without supervisor approval—to correct a hotel guest's problem.[13] Other types of companies offer a similar approach. Whole Foods Market, the grocery chain, has teams interview and select their new coworkers to make sure they fit.[14] The philosophy of Patagonia, the outdoor clothing company, shapes the way it operates, and its employees gravitate to its values-based standards, manifested in everything from on-site child care to open communication to environmentally friendly products.[15] Thus each of these firms transforms its values into a unique customer experience.

The main point is that the Incubate practice of cultivating the talent in your company creates sustainable performance and flexibility of execution, whereas the other three profiles are more vulnerable to burnout or stagnation. Your employees' ability to create an experience or a solution for the customer is worth more than any product because markets can change and make your strategies worthless. Organizations often cut employee quality first, but the ability to create new value resides in high-potential employees. For example, Intel's *ability* to make a chip is what makes it a valuable company, not the specific chips it produces, which are obsolete within months. When you hire the best, you can sit back and watch what happens. You may not know in advance what outcomes you will get, but you know for certain that they have the capacity to produce and sustain value into the future.

■ Tool: Talent Scouting ■

Desired Outcomes
- Find, develop, and retain the best people.
- Establish a sustainable high-performing culture.
- Share values.
- Create a collaborative work environment where people are encouraged to learn from their mistakes.

Time Needed
- Frequency: Ongoing.

Setting
- Hiring people: Anywhere in the world where there are potential new hires.
- Orienting and developing people: Wherever new hires can be placed to learn from peers and mentors.

Materials
- A company mission and values statement should drive the hiring and development process.

Who Should Participate
- Everyone in your firm who will work with new hires.

Facilitation
- Leaders and managers with an understanding of the values and objectives of your organization.

Steps of the Process

Determine Your "People" Needs
- Use the creativity assessment (Chapter Two) to assess the strengths and gaps represented by your current team. Use the creativity map to consider your team's capabilities and how it needs to be built and expanded. (For more ideas on how to use the map for this purpose, see Chapter Seven.)

Find Potentially Creative People
- To find high-potential people with values, skills, and experience that are right for your firm, look for people who
  - Work in an environment with values like yours.

■ Tool: Talent Scouting, Cont'd ■

- ▪ Have successfully been a member of another group or team.
- ▪ Have worked on initiatives like those in your organization.
- ▪ Have had to teach others how to do what they do well.
- ▪ Have an active, non-work lifestyle interest that relates to your company's values (for example, Sierra Club, volunteering, church).
- ▪ Are currently customers who are passionate about your products or services.
- ▪ Remember to look inside your firm, too!

Test for the Right Abilities
- ▪ As part of the evaluation process, ask each candidate to spend some time working or meeting with the team.
- ▪ Afterward, ask the candidate some probing questions:
  - ▪ Describe what you see in the team:
    - ▪ What works? Why do you think that is?
    - ▪ What doesn't work? Why is that?
  - ▪ What experiences do you have with a team like this one?
  - ▪ What types of initiatives and teams would you like to be associated with?
  - ▪ If you were brought into this team tomorrow:
    - ▪ What values and skills would you bring to the team? How would they be complementary? How would they be different?
    - ▪ How would you develop a sufficient understanding of the team and their work?
    - ▪ What would motivate you to be a high performer on this team?
    - ▪ How would you establish your credibility with the team?
    - ▪ How would you develop yourself to be of greater service to the team?
    - ▪ What changes and improvements to the team would you suggest?
    - ▪ How would you help the team make these changes and improvements?
- ▪ Contact the candidate's references and see if they will tell you more about how the candidate's past work supports and extends the answers to these interview questions.
- ▪ After the candidate leaves, ask the team what they thought. The final decision is the team's. Not only will they have to work with whoever you hire, but the new hire will appreciate being "chosen" by the group.

Rewarding Creativity
- ▪ No single reward will fit everyone's needs or motivate every type of employee. A "cafeteria approach," where individuals each work out their own rewards with their manager and team, is far preferable for giving employees incentives that they truly value.[16]
- ▪ Consider non-pay incentives that might appeal to different employees, because individuals with different creativity profiles may prize different incentives. For example:

□

■ Tool: Talent Scouting, Cont'd ■

- Imagine: An ever-changing stream of new opportunities to express themselves and design new projects, with a reward of a high degree of freedom.
- Invest: Important opportunities to solve difficult problems and overcome barriers to success, with a reward of increased pay and power.
- Improve: Opportunities to improve processes and establish order, with a reward of increased responsibilities and promotion.
- Incubate: Opportunities to build relationships and learn from admired mentors, with a reward of increased personal development.
- Consider also offering rewards in the form of ideal working conditions. (See Chapter Seven for more information on this point.)

Orient New Hires Adequately
- Don't be content with a boilerplate orientation session for new employees. Orient new hires by apprenticing them to advisers who exemplify your company's values and practices.
- In addition to helping immerse the new hire in the firm's culture, an adviser or "learning buddy" may be helpful in identifying potential improvement points in the new hire's development. This continuous learning loop should be encouraging and supportive.
- After an initial period of orientation, it may be useful to put multiple new hires in groups of peers. These colleagues become a cohort that will develop together. This approach can reinforce the values and practices of the community on all sides. One risk, however, is that such groups can grow disconnected from others in the organization.
- Shared language, symbols, and rituals can help establish a sense of ownership for core values and practices. The caution here is to avoid overdoing it—you don't want groups to develop their own identity to the exclusion or repulsion of others.

Encourage the Growth of New Competencies
- Make people development a key component of your employees' job descriptions. Regularly ask employees what new competencies they've helped to develop in their subordinates and fellow team members. Consider hiring someone whose specific job is to foster this behavior in your organization.
- Consider the balance of roles a creative project or ongoing function requires when assigning team members to particular tasks, responsibilities, or phases of a project. See Chapters Two and Seven for more information about the preferences and work settings that appeal to different profiles.
- People develop new skills not by doing what they know how to do but by trying to do what they don't. One effective way to develop people is to

■ Tool: Talent Scouting, Cont'd ■

put them on creative projects as soon as they are hired. This is not a "trial by fire" to see who survives but rather an opportunity to accelerate the development of new skills by giving people a chance to learn from failures.

- Assign projects to small groups who are free to do what is necessary and who are responsible for producing results. Consider treating projects like small businesses with a charter, budget, timeline, and deliverables. Let the team members develop competency, excitement, and ownership for their work.

Encourage People to Challenge Boundaries
- High-potential people need to expand their boundaries and those of the firm. Moreover, trial-and-error experiments often improve business practices, as long as people learn from their mistakes and share their lessons. Encourage risk taking and avoid imposing control structures that deny high-potential hires the experiences they need to grow.
- For this to succeed, give your new hires slack in terms of time, space, resources, and the opportunity to improvise.

Source: From *Creativity at Work* by Jeff DeGraff and Katherine A. Lawrence. Copyright © 2002 by John Wiley & Sons.

Capsule Overview: Idea Spaces

What idea spaces are . . .
Places that help employees cultivate and share knowledge.

An idea space can be a discrete location and a sanctuary from workplace distractions, but often organizations that value idea spaces have a commitment to a pervasive idea space environment. Space is not only physical but also mental. Dislocating the typical task-oriented work mode helps people gain the freedom of mind and insight necessary to produce great ideas.

What idea spaces get you . . . Employees
with the versatility and energy necessary for their work.

The right idea space can stretch, develop, encourage, and motivate. Idea spaces create places for like-minded people to share insights and leverage learning within and across the company's internal boundaries. Idea spaces can become storage places where knowledge can be passed on to future generations of employees. Employees who gather there are routinely learning from experiments. Eventually, their newly developed competencies result in opportunities for creating new products and services.

What idea spaces don't get you . . .
Predictable results.

Chaos is both the benefit and the disadvantage of idea spaces. As with the cultivation of people, the results from the use of idea spaces are neither quantifiable nor, typically, fast. It is impossible to demand new knowledge or capacities in the same way that you outline investment targets. Moreover, it is not easy to know when a necessary competency is ripe, so pinpointing the readiness to start a new project is difficult. Ultimately, the results of idea spaces are divergent (producing a variety of ideas or capabilities), so they will not necessarily center on a predetermined market need.

When idea spaces work best . . .
You need a sustainable flow of new ideas and
employees with the know-how to generate them.

The long-term benefits of idea spaces are realized through ongoing, sustainable nourishment of your workforce. They work best when the people who work in them are empowered, involved, and strongly motivated to collaborate and develop a knowledge-sharing community. The company must also be committed to offering slack time or resources (such as learning programs and sabbaticals). In short, this tool is most useful when a company's people are its strategy.

Case Study: A Hallmark of Idea Spaces

Once upon a time, in a land far, far away (well, Kansas City, Missouri, in the mid-1980s), there was a great storyteller and seer named Gordon MacKenzie.[17] He plied his trade creating cards for Hallmark, a greeting card empire. MacKenzie likened Hallmark to a giant hairball—a massive tangle of corporate normalcy, formed of past decisions, procedures, and policies that entangled all minds within it. To be creatively productive, MacKenzie realized it was necessary to distance oneself from the entanglements of the hairball without disconnecting from the spirit of the corporate mission that would provide the focus for creativity.

One day, MacKenzie proposed establishing a creative studio called the Humor Workshop. It was to operate like a small, independent business that served Hallmark. MacKenzie asked his new recruits to describe their fantasy of a perfect studio. The result was this: Each artist and writer was furnished with an antique rolltop desk. Their personal workspaces were separated by stained-glass windows and beveled-glass doors hung from the ceiling with rope. More doors hinged together created portable privacy screens. Each desk had a rustic milk can as a wastebasket. The final cost of the décor was 17 percent less expensive than a standard cubicle farm, yet provided a rich and stimulating enclave for his artists to work together. It was so appealing that a continuous stream of other employees came by to see if the rumors were true.

A few years later, MacKenzie reinvented himself and his work environment again. His boss asked him to take a new position as a "burr in his saddle."[18] Though this assignment was anything but specific, MacKenzie decided that his role was to endorse great ideas that were stuck in the system. He gave himself the job title "Creative Paradox" and created an atmosphere suitable for the mysterious nature of his position. He altered the standard office lighting to create a mystical mood and covered his walls with large paintings of Chinese calligraphy and cryptic sayings. He found a wild sculpture made from a brightly painted wooden chair with angel wings and a halo sprouting from the back. He hung the chair at a 45-degree angle from the ceiling, just above his own work chair, "to give the impression that I'd recently slid out of it and dropped down to earth."[19] It was here that he welcomed other employees who came to him to share their new ideas. In turn, he would affirm that their ideas were good. *Every one of them.*

Today, Hallmark continues to encourage idea spaces for "creative renewal." Next door to its headquarters, the company has a giant innovation facility full of studios for crafts such as glass blowing, ceramics, and papermaking. Outside Kansas City, the company maintains a farmhouse-turned-artist-studio for woodworking, blacksmithing, and other crafts. These activities allow employees to take a few hours' or even a few months' break to get away from their work and rejuvenate their spark.

Hallmark also sponsors its employees on longer sabbaticals to learn about social trends. They travel the country, doing hands-on research on such topics as ethnicity, computer technology, and death and dying. They return from their sabbaticals brimming with product ideas and share their experiences with their colleagues. Employees feel the lasting effects of invigoration and transformation from their sabbaticals, and their energy and fresh ideas help sustain Hallmark as a leading producer of greeting cards and year-round gifts.

■ Discussion: The Pleasures of Idea Spaces

The Hallmark story illustrates how companies can encourage people to stretch their minds and their knowledge through attention to the space in which creativity happens. *Space* in this context includes mental as well as physical space. In fact, what the "office" is, how it is designed, where it is situated, and when work happens are important factors to consider when creating an idea space.

The "what." Physical space matters. Colors and lighting, scents, sounds, and layout—all have effects on our alertness, blood pressure, judgment, energy levels, and interaction with others.[20] In fact, aspects of office design have been found to affect job performance, job satisfaction, and communication to the degree that a well-designed space can improve productivity by as much as 15 percent.[21] Firms that offer facilities to help other companies with product or idea development (such as IDEO, the Eureka Ranch, or the knOwhere Store) pay particular attention to creating a stimulating environment.[22]

The "how." At Hallmark, MacKenzie asked his designers what would be an ideal environment for them to work in—and made it so. More and more frequently, companies recognize that people have to work in the way that they work best. For example, IDEO, a leading design firm, encourages employees to customize their work environment. They surround themselves with materials, tools, and reminders of past inventions that will help them do their work. IDEO's leaders value such efforts because they recognize that their largest investment is in people. As IDEO's general manager Tom Kelley says, "Why shouldn't you pay the same attention to how you create the spaces in which this talent must perform? Athletes need proper facilities. Why not workers?"[23] Idea spaces are places that employees can shape to fit their needs and, more important, that will invite them to develop their ideas and knowledge.

The "where." Hallmark sends people around the country to learn new things. The company also has built off-site retreats where employees can try new activities. Great ideas surface from social interactions with others who can provide a fresh perspective, even those we meet by chance.[24] However, people interact with those they find easiest to meet. Someone who sits a few steps away is several times more likely to be consulted for an idea than someone who sits six or seven offices down the hall. Research has shown that a distance of more than seventy-five feet drops the likelihood of interaction to nearly zero.[25] Some organizations overcome this problem by fostering opportunities for people to meet colleagues and interact with new people: installing a "town center" or a café, locating basic resources like printers and copiers in a central location, or making staff kitchens or hallways inviting places to meet. Proximity makes invention born from cross-fertilization of ideas more likely.

The "when." Creativity, particularly in the Incubate quadrant, is unpredictable in its duration and arrival. Hallmark recognizes the value of time devoted to "percolating" new ideas. MacKenzie has pointed out that the majority of creativity happens invisibly, during quiet time. As with cows making milk, only a portion of employees' time actually *looks* productive, yet managers concerned with productivity often expect employees to be doing something—anything—or else it seems like they are not working. Likewise, David Kelley, founder of IDEO, believes that sitting at one's desk is not necessarily the best way to generate ideas.[26] Instead, creativity frequently happens at unexpected moments: when doing nothing, having a new experience, or doing mindless work.[27] By providing idea spaces, companies create a place for people to be creative when they are feeling creative.

Making the world your office. Hallmark offers an additional resource to its employees: a place away from their home base. Hallmark does this in two ways. It sends people on sabbaticals, and it provides "creative renewal" opportunities.

The first important resource is encouraging employees to physically get away from the home office. Hallmark recognizes that new ideas—underrepresented consumer markets, a new technology, a new way of doing something, or spotting what is in fashion—are likely to be found in the world at large, not in the office. By living in a new place among different people, employees are able to dislocate from the typical work mode. Thus, these sabbaticals give people the permission to try something they would not try at home—and they can return to inject some of their inspiration back into the company by initiating new product lines.

The second resource is Hallmark's "creative renewal" studios. These craft studios are more than just a place to relax—they represent the mental space needed to step away from the assumptions and obstructions of headquarters. The employees enter a refreshing place where they can think new thoughts or learn new things. Also, hierarchies and routines are sidelined when people come to a neutral location that is away from their usual offices.

■ Using Idea Spaces: Cultivating a Community for Knowledge Sharing

Companies such as Hallmark recognize that people—and their knowledge and abilities—are their most valuable asset. By creating a specific space that is conducive to sharing knowledge and ideas, they amplify the benefits of investing in the individual. Thus the key value of an idea space is that it allows people to connect, build rapport, and share their expertise.

This social learning system is commonly called a *community of practice*.[28] In communities of practice, members of the community exchange ideas, tell stories, and share ways of working. These joint experiences help illuminate both the tacit and explicit day-to-day knowledge that practitioners use, and together they create new knowledge.[29] Eventually, the firm becomes more than the sum of the individuals because together they have a common place to tap into their resources.

The specific community space offers a way for knowledge to be shared, retained, and passed to newcomers, even as employees move to new positions at the firm and elsewhere. In contrast, when workers are isolated from each other, particular kinds of problems tend to be assigned to the one person known to handle that type of problem. Over time, experts become "towers of knowledge" who never have the opportunity to share their expertise with others. When one of these towers leaves the organization, all their expertise leaves with them.[30] By contrast, when firms create communities of practice, they ensure that knowledge is enhanced and exchanged throughout the organization and prevent any single departure from leaving a debilitating gap.

Community is also a conduit for invention. Spending time together fosters an emotional, intangible foundation for work relationships. As people connect, ideas begin to cascade beyond the confines of the space. For example, Silicon Valley was the home of the Internet boom because technologists had been gathering in that part of the country for years. Some of the earliest advances had been born there, and special interest groups had supported the development of many of the core software technologies. In addition, on-line venues such as the Well helped ideas spread to those limited by geography. Networking, both literal and figurative, became the source of new ideas and business ventures.[31]

Admittedly, those who have to answer to shareholders or deadlines might find it difficult to understand or accept the value produced by idea spaces. Although they cannot produce certain, specific results, idea spaces are one of the best ways to sustain and enable future creativity that will have bottom-line effects. Rather than expecting some*thing* to emerge, idea spaces help produce people—employees or clients—who know how to be creative. By expressing themselves, growing a new talent, or collaborating with others, these people become more valuable because they will have the skills and ideas to make their customers happier or provide better service.

Like talent scouting, idea spaces can create a culture or a subculture within an organization.[32] Strong organizational cultures can have many benefits, such as creating a sense of stability and continuity, social norms, and a common identity.[33] Employees who flourish in a particular culture, particularly when emotions are strong, are often more committed to their organizations.[34] Moreover, some repeat customers are drawn to a particular company by the consistency of experience that a defined culture enables. Although organizational culture is a complex phenomenon, the two tools in this chapter suggest ways that employees can nurture a culture that serves them best.

How a workplace is organized physically speaks volumes about how work is done and how the organization values creativity. This tool will help you create and sustain an idea space of your own.

■ Tool: Idea Spaces ■

Desired Outcomes
- Provide a sanctuary from institutional thinking.
- Give employees a place to free their minds and develop creative thinking ability.
- Offer a "test track" to experiment with new ideas.
- Develop communities of practice for sharing knowledge and experience.

Time Needed
- Planning and setup: A new idea space could take a week or less to establish, provided that the space is available, but to be successful the space must evolve over time.
- Frequency of use: Aim to organize "official events" monthly, but encourage continuous use.

Setting
- A place that is easily accessible from the office, but away from its daily activities (phone calls, e-mail, and other distractions of office life). Good lighting, pleasant décor, comfortable furniture, and room for spreading out is helpful.

Materials
- Artifacts that stimulate new associations: toys, art supplies, interesting knick-knacks, artwork, musical instruments, music, and magazines. Creativity software and the Internet may be helpful in stimulating new ideas.
- Tools to record and share ideas: white boards, sticky notes, flip charts, computer terminals, video cameras, and voice recorders.

Who Should Participate
- Planning and setup: Anyone can help with the initial setup of the space, but you should consider it open to ongoing evolution and feedback from those who use it.
- Ongoing use: Any individual or group with a need to either get away from "corporate" thinking for a while or generate some new ideas in a stimulating setting.

Facilitation
- Ideally, there should be someone who is responsible for the space. This person could help people network, find specialists, or locate information resources.
- Consider grooming someone for the role of brainstorming facilitator on an "as needed" basis.
- If your budget is small, at least make sure someone keeps the space clean and appealing.

■ Tool: Idea Spaces, Cont'd ■

Steps of the Process

Determine the Outcomes
- In addition to encouraging a community of practice, decide what other reasons you might want to use this space. Consider the items listed as "Desired Outcomes" at the start of this tool.

Give the Space a Metaphor or Theme
- A metaphor or theme can shape how people will think about and use this space. Themes like "kitchen of the mind" or "corporate garage" quickly express their real purpose to the uninitiated participant. Use this theme to develop the physical space, as you would a theme restaurant, and the activities associated with it. Try themes on intended user groups before giving the space a name to see what connects with them, or you might even want to wait until the space has been created and used.

Construct the Physical Space
- Location and resource constraints are the first factors to consider when selecting a space. If the budget is limited, try to find a space already owned or leased by the firm, or convert an existing space with a "lab-on-demand" approach. The lab doesn't have to be at the workplace; you can locate it in a house or other nontraditional space.
- Consider all the needs of the space: functional, aesthetic, audiovisual, information. Be prepared to support needs that emerge from the activities of the users.
- Remember that people need to be both relaxed and stimulated in the space, so it needs to be both comfortable and interesting—aesthetics matter.
- Provide ways that ideas can be displayed or archived where others can draw upon them for inspiration and improve the ideas.

Create the Experience
- The aim of the physical space is to create mental space for the people who use it. It must become a sanctuary from conventional company thinking. Activities within the space must therefore emphasize the breaking of daily task pursuits such as phone calls, to-do lists, e-mail, and meetings. To create this freedom from the daily grind, a time-out from routine activities must be strictly observed. Personal techniques such as meditation, deep breathing, or physical stretching exercises may help people move out of their normal "work mode."

■ Tool: Idea Spaces, Cont'd ■

Attract and Assemble Communities
- Determine what will bring specific communities of practice to this space. Is it location, certain projects, topics of interest, or a common occupation?
- Promote a clear yet flexible code of conduct (brainstorming rules, expected responsibilities, and the like).
- In this space, conversation is the content. The more diverse and capable the people who use the space, the more likely something of value will result. Every bright idea created and problem solved in turn has the potential to become a new or improved product or service.
- Encourage participants to bring real-world issues into their conversations. The space isn't just for wild imagining—it's also for discussing and solving real problems and challenges associated with the company's products or services.

Establish the Processes
- The theme of the idea space will influence the processes that groups should use. For example, the theme of an "idea factory" encourages treating the space as an accelerator that transforms breakthrough ideas into new product design and development processes. In contrast, a "boot camp" metaphor may focus more on teaching creativity techniques and developing esprit de corps.
- Idea space processes may be of many types, but often fall into one of four categories:
  - Stimulation: To stimulate people's imagination through new interactions. *Examples:* Art, music, dance, field trips, and sabbaticals.
  - Facilitation: To assist small groups as a seasoned "travel guide" for their journey toward breakthrough ideas and action. *Examples:* Facilitating jump-start creativity processes or hosting the work of communities of practice.
  - Experimentation: To provide a workshop or laboratory for the development of ideas into products, services, and learning. *Examples:* Virtual labs, idea banks, incubators, and accelerators.
  - Education: To develop creativity competencies in individuals and groups through teaching, partnership, and mentoring. *Examples:* Creative thinking methods training, learning partnerships, and mentoring.
- These processes may be custom designed for the space or they may integrate existing processes that the specific community of practice already uses.

Learn and Communicate
- Regularly ask the people who use the space, "What have we learned?"
- Consider enlisting thought leaders, experts, business leaders, and peers to discuss and review (with the participants themselves) the

---

■ Tool: Idea Spaces, Cont'd ■

---

activities and experiments that have been generated in the space. This review can

- Provide access to key sources of information, relevant data, and experience, and communicate it effectively to other practitioners.
- Allow the review group to creatively think about potential new approaches and solutions to problems and barriers with a diverse group of people without collecting a lot of data in advance.
- Uncover good ideas that were overlooked.
- Yield an informed account of the relative success of the space as well as ideas for potential improvements.

- Getting responses from others about the things you have been learning can be helpful. Conferences or learning fairs are sometimes useful in communicating key findings to larger groups. A virtual space on the Internet is a good way to do this, too.

Source: From *Creativity at Work* by Jeff DeGraff and Katherine A. Lawrence. Copyright © 2002 by John Wiley & Sons.

CHAPTER SUMMARY

The Incubate profile pursues sustainable creativity by finding and nurturing people in the best possible environment. The practices are best suited for situations that need internally focused systems to produce divergent solutions. Through talent scouting and idea spaces, companies in this profile hope to create community and share knowledge.

Talent scouting is selecting high-potential people with the right attitude and basic skills and giving them experiences to support their growth. Employees become versatile and capable, supporting a strong culture that centers around values. However, this approach relies on an environment that allows managers to make hiring decisions and empower their employees to learn by doing.

Idea spaces are places that help employees cultivate and share knowledge. Whether an off-site retreat or a central gathering room, an idea space allows employees to interact with others and think in new ways. Idea spaces are best in firms that are willing to provide the slack time and resources to produce results that will not be predictable or quantifiable.

The practices in the Incubate profile require management to value long-term rewards and recognize that their employees are their greatest asset.

Putting It Together

Guiding, Managing, and Integrating Creativity

The four creativity profiles may function independently, but the real art of creativity management and leadership is in blending the profiles. You will probably need to manage the inherent tensions among multiple profiles to achieve the purposes of your work situation.

The ideas in this chapter apply to all levels of management. Every manager's realm is both a whole in itself and part of something larger, responsive to the demands of both insiders and outsiders. Whether your managerial position is at the top or somewhere in the middle, you can use the creativity map to guide, manage, and integrate creativity practices within your sphere of responsibility.

If you are a mid-level manager, you may wonder how you could possibly have the authority or control to implement creativity practices in your organization. You may have little say in creating the strategy of your firm or minimal access to extensive resources for developing wide-ranging creativity practices. You are probably focused on some particular function or task that creativity could enhance—but can you really change what happens in your area of the firm?

The fact is that every unit in a firm—no matter how big or small—faces challenges that demand creativity and can use the tools we have provided in this book. For example, as a manager, you could adapt the forecasting tool used by Reuters (Chapter Three) to engage various operating groups in developing strategic foresight to bring your team to a shared vision of the future. The method is the same; all that changes is the organizational unit to which it is applied.

You can also use the creativity map to understand how the forces operating on the firm affect your decision-making options. For example, if your firm had a bad quarter and investors are unhappy, you know that your firm's chief priority is to create profits. This is characteristic of the Invest profile, and the logical response for the firm as a whole is to take actions that are in line with Invest practices. At the same time, within your area of responsibility—say, in coming up with radically new marketing initiatives—you may need to move more in the direction of Imagine practices. Such tensions are an inherent part of creativity management. Once you understand the dynamics affecting your particular situation, you can focus on the specific things you should be doing as a manager within the broader context of the challenges facing the firm.

In this chapter, we discuss how to identify and develop the right blend of practices for your part of your organization. We will guide you through three exercises that address your primary decisions:

- Setting your direction
- Creating an action plan to integrate appropriate creativity practices
- Developing the creative ability you need

■ Setting Your Direction

Setting direction for your organization, unit, or team can be a challenge when you consider the multiple, competing purposes and priorities in your organization. It's important to understand the tensions you'll inevitably face as you try to plot your direction—and how these tensions can actually enhance creativity.

Finding the Right Mix

Rarely, if ever, should an organization, a unit, or even an individual rely on only one type of creativity. Life just isn't that simple. As you've seen throughout this book, the creativity practices you need to use depend on the outcomes you want. To avoid being trapped in the extremes of one creativity profile, successful leaders draw on other profiles for balance. They may do so in the course of everyday business or over time. Inevitably there will be tensions among the preferences and customary practices of groups and individuals who align themselves with one or another type of creativity—between, say, the product designers who tend to operate in the Imagine profile and the manufacturing engineers who focus on controlling quality through Improve practices.

Tension is usually associated with stress, but the tensions that result from diversity are among the keys to productive creativity in an organization. Tension between the profiles produces energy and vigorous debate. For example, human resource departments perpetually argue the case for more spending on training as a long-term investment in employees, while finance departments counter with the need to produce quick, profitable outcomes by cutting costs that don't meet short-term needs. Healthy organizations, like families, don't always agree. From these differences come new perspectives. The organization that does not allow new ideas to enter is unlikely to create anything of value.

Diversity is the *real* secret formula of creativity. Unfortunately, industry sectors, cultures, and geographical regions often have strong inclinations toward one of the four creativity profiles because value is defined for them by their markets, shareholders, products, and services. Like most individuals who are right- or left-handed, they can learn to be ambidextrous, but they probably will always have a dominant hand that they use for highly skilled work. However, by developing a weak profile to be stronger or by integrating two opposing profiles, organizations create better competencies and outcomes. For example, large Improve-minded chemical companies are buying small Imagine-oriented life sciences firms in an attempt to create differentiated designer chemicals in large volumes.

To produce winning products, services, and processes, a firm needs all creative competencies, but these competencies tend to be overlaid by the character of the organization's dominant approach. A prime example of this mix is Corning, the world's top producer of fiber-optic cable and an industry leader in high-tech optical and display materials and components.[1] Its huge manufacturing volumes of standardized components suggest that its dominant profile is Improve. Yet Corning has created a multifaceted approach to creativity at its Sullivan Park research laboratories.[2] There Corning integrates free-thinking artistry with tough-minded scientific research. It has a formal five-step innovation review process (Invest-style portfolio management), constant informal communication (an Incubate value), a requirement for scientists to spend 10 percent of their time pursuing wild ideas (Imagine-type exploration), and careful attention to staffing projects with the right people to solve the problem (Improve's systematic structuring). This synthesis has been a key to its success.

When you move in one direction on the creativity map (say, toward big or fast creativity), you ordinarily move away from another (for example, small or slow). However, as Corning demonstrates, you can move in all directions simultaneously—but only if you are extremely careful to balance the approaches and direct each competency toward different outcomes. Moving toward any extreme requires you to put some of your efforts into implementing practices that reflect the opposite profile. With such measures, you can safely and effectively diversify your creativity practices.

Developing range in how you create is an exercise in awareness, skill, and desire. By identifying your organization's favored creativity profile and the favored profiles of specific functional areas, work groups, and individuals, you will inevitably generate some tensions. View these differences with respect, and allow diversity to create value.

Mapping the Purposes of Specific Groups

Ultimately, setting direction is about focus—it is about what you decide *not* to do. Trying to do everything will, in the end, accomplish nothing. Instead, develop the practices that support your top priorities.

One way of setting direction is to map the purposes of your group (by which we mean any structural unit within the organization, including the organization itself). To do this, you must ask yourself a few key questions:

- Where are we now?
- Where do we need to go?
- What do we need to do to get there?

To help answer these questions, first consider the overall purposes of the organization, and then consider the purposes sought by the business unit within which your own group operates. For example, if you manage a human resource group within a manufacturing unit, your group may be pursuing Incubate purposes while the other parts of the operation are pursuing Improve purposes. Your efforts may or may not need to be better aligned with the next larger business unit, but either way, recognizing the differences will clarify your goals. To find out what purposes your organization or business unit is actually pursuing—whatever its publicly stated mission might be—pay close attention to where resources are invested and what creativity competencies and practices the members have developed. These are clues that reveal what kinds of purposes (that is, outcomes) are really being pursued.

Second, consider the purposes sought by the subgroups within your own group. Again, it helps to examine where they put their resources and what competencies they have developed. If your firm doesn't have hierarchical levels, consider the units that are upstream and downstream from you in your business process.

Third, reflect on your own group's current biases and tendencies. You will likely want to involve other members of your group for this activity. You can use the creativity assessment presented in Chapter Two as an aid in revealing the profiles of the people in your group and the practices of the group as a whole.

Finally, summarize the purposes that your group needs to pursue in each profile to achieve the blend of outcomes desired, and plot these purposes on the creativity map. The map provides a single image that represents where you are and where you want to go with your creativity practices. In setting your direction, consider whether the role of your group is to counterbalance other groups in your organization or to be aligned with them by sharing the same purposes. Number the four profiles according to your priorities. Your first (and possibly second) priority sets your primary direction. The example in Exhibit 7.1 shows a group that wants to move toward the top of the map in an effort to achieve greater flexibility.

Exhibit 7.1. Example of Using the Creativity Map to Analyze Group Needs

Divergent

Incubate 1	**Imagine** 2
Where are we now?	**Where are we now?**
We lack a culture to support creativity.	We have great ideas that we never develop.
Where do we want to go?	**Where do we want to go?**
Leaders who consider creativity as a primary part of their agenda.	Give breakthrough ideas a chance to be tested.
What do we need to do to get there?	**What do we need to do to get there?**
Fully utilize the creative potential of our people.	Leaders willing to break with the party line.
Hire people for their creative abilities.	Processes that make a place for high-risk, high-potential ideas.
Improve 3	**Invest** 4
Where are we now?	**Where are we now?**
We have strong processes and systems for creating minor product variations.	Effective process for advancing ideas with high potential for success.
Where do we want to go?	**Where do we want to go?**
Allow flexibility in the early stages of product development.	Loosen up some funding for a few out-of-the-box ideas.
What do we need to do to get there?	**What do we need to do to get there?**
Make a place for creative thinking in the project planning process.	Change the resource allocation scheme.
	More partnering with other departments and firms.

Internal   *External*

Direction

Convergent

In this example, the group has examined each profile in the creativity map and asked, "Where are we now?" "Where do we need to go?" and "What do we need to do to get there?" Next, they summarized their purposes and plotted them according to each profile. Finally, they ranked the four profiles in terms of priority. The fact that the upper two quadrants in the map received the highest rankings indicates that the group should focus on moving toward practices that encourage a divergent approach—that is, toward increasing flexibility.

You can use shapes, lines, colors, symbols, and words that are meaningful to you when you create your map. A picture is often more potent than a written statement because it is easily remembered. Keep it simple. Hang this map someplace where it can be seen and discussed by everyone in your group.

■ Creating an Action Plan: Integrating Appropriate Creativity Practices

Now that you've set the direction for your unit or team, you need to figure out what creativity practices are right for you and create an action plan for initiating and integrating diverse practices. Of course, you may already have several different practices at work in your organization or unit. This next exercise will help you take those existing practices into account as you decide what you would like to change or initiate. First, however, you should know about three possible barriers to implementing the direction you have set.

Barriers to Implementation

Implementing an integrated approach to creativity isn't necessarily a straightforward process. Along the way, you may encounter incompatible purposes and practices: negative zones, and multiple purposes and practices that act as barriers.

Incompatible Purposes and Practices. A unit or team may have competencies or employ practices that are incompatible with their desired purposes. When these practices are highly developed, they can become detrimental. For example, *quality* is typically achieved through the rigorous use of process and technology controls to reduce errors. In contrast, *growth* is frequently the result of speculation and a wide array of marketing trial and error; indeed, growth can come from launching in multiple markets and seeing which ones work. These purposes require practices that employ opposite methods. If one set of practices or competencies is more highly valued, then the opposite purpose will become marginalized.

It is important to understand what creativity practices you and your team use and what results these practices are likely to produce. If your practices and purposes are not aligned, you must choose between developing new practices or redefining your desired results.

Negative Zones. Sometimes an organization or group will develop its strongest practices to such an extreme that they become liabilities.[3] Practices taken too far move them from zones of positive to negative performance:

- Imagine practices taken too far lead to unrelated products and services or products that cannot be manufactured effectively.
- Invest practices taken too far lead to a series of short-term projects that lack long-term commitment and the ability to sustain them.
- Improve practices taken too far become a bureaucratic system of controls that stifle the development of different ideas.
- Incubate practices taken too far become a community that values its own mission and beliefs over its obligations to customers and shareholders.

Determine if your group might be operating in the negative zone and consider ways of modifying its practices. Increasing the quantity or extent of your practices in the opposite profile on the creativity map can sometimes remedy this imbalance.

Multiple Purposes and Practices. Most organizations and groups want to accomplish everything well. However, there is an inverse relationship between the number of goals and the amount of attention, resources, and vigor available to pursue any of them. The greater the number of purposes, the less attention is available for each. To resolve this dilemma, organizations or groups can choose to pursue multiple purposes in one of three ways: *separation, sequencing,* or *synthesis.*

First, an organization may pursue different purposes and operate separately across departments, locations, or business units. For example, the managers of a large-scale manufacturing plant may aim for optimization, while the operating director overseeing that business line may aim for profits. Their competing aims can either balance each other, meaning each is pursued more moderately than if everyone was pursuing a single outcome, or the aims can interfere with each other as their advocates pursue conflicting organizational agendas. An organization that does not seek to integrate its functions and units may create fewer synergies, but the advantage is that each part of the organization will be relatively unencumbered by creativity practices that do not fit the unit's unique purposes. For example, a new product development group would not need to observe documentation requirements; instead, such issues would be addressed when the product moves to the manufacturing division.

Second, different purposes may be pursued sequentially. Over the life cycle of a project, a product, or the firm, the purposes of creativity will change. It is important to regularly assess where you are in the process and choose creativity practices that match the current purposes. For example, at the start of a new project, a company may be in hot pursuit of a new technology—the purpose of innovation. As the project matures, the focus shifts to manufacturing with optimal resource usage—the purpose of optimization. The competencies needed to create these results need to be adjusted accordingly. Similarly, the most effective project managers at the beginning will need to either manage the project differently at later stages or transfer the project to different managers when the needed type of creativity changes.

Third, the most versatile organizations are capable of synthesizing opposing purposes. In fact, there is mounting evidence that those organizations that can simultaneously hold multiple purposes are more likely to increase their market value.[4] For example, Sony has made its reputation on highly innovative products (an Imagine strength) that also offer good quality (Improve). In such cases, the firm and its leaders must develop the ability to manage paradoxes. The separate and contrasting needs of each purpose are recognized and supported through the development of appropriate practices and competencies.

This kind of synthesis is not easy to do. Most people with a strong bias toward one profile cannot see how another perspective can be incorporated. This is why, for most organizations, choosing a purpose and the associated practices is about trade-offs—discarding three profiles and focusing on one. Both separation and sequencing are forms of trade-off thinking. Corning, however, exemplifies an alternative: an integration of multiple profiles. Integration involves retaining one's dominant profile while accommodating one or more other profiles.

It is important to distinguish accommodation from assimilation. Accommodation means adapting another profile to your purposes while retaining its distinctive strengths. In some cases, people are able to see the value of another profile, but they end up assimilating the unfamiliar profile into their own so that it does not retain the qualities that make it valuable. For example, reengineering was an attempt of Improve-minded people to draw on the Imagine profile and increase innovation within the boundaries of quality or optimization. Unfortunately, reengineering tended to squash all of what would have been different from the Improve perspective, leaving only the intention of innovation without the tools to achieve it.

In contrast, those rare people who can accommodate other profiles view their activities from a perspective that is not as heavily biased by their dominant profile. Two terrific examples are Buckminster Fuller and Walt Disney. Although Fuller was a solid Improve-minded engineer, he wanted to consider how engineering could solve future problems, an Imagine type of thinking. Likewise, Disney, whose vision associates him with the Imagine profile, acknowledged that addressing issues of scale and capacity (Improve) would help him create his dream world of tomorrow. Thus, Fuller engineered answers for questions that didn't yet exist, while Disney imagined a future that would need engineered solutions to achieve it.

Integration is the most promising path to high-value creativity, because it allows you to reap the benefits of the practices from other profiles while staying true to your top priorities. See Exhibit 7.2 for examples of how integration works.

Developing Your Action Plan

To integrate practices from different creativity profiles in your own situation, your team (or unit or division) needs to draw on the diversity of each profile separately before combining the perspectives into an action plan. To do so, use the following three-step process:

1. Consider how to achieve your purposes by generating many ideas.
2. Identify the potential solution that you like best and the profile that it represents. Consider the solution from the perspective of the other profiles, and look for hybrid possibilities.
3. Identify what action you'll take on the basis of these other perspectives.

Gather members of your group together for this activity. You'll need a space where you can brainstorm and post ideas where everyone in the group can see them as you go through

Exhibit 7.2. **Examples of Integrating Creativity Practices**

Incubate	Imagine
Purpose: Sustainable community and knowledge *Integrated practices:* - *Imagine:* Train people to think out of the box. - *Invest:* Establish shared values around tangibly improving performance. - *Improve:* Mentor people to develop manufacturing expertise.	*Purpose:* New innovations and vision *Integrated practices:* - *Invest:* Design with the goal of demonstrating quick, tangible results. - *Improve:* Invent within the boundaries of an industry or platform standard. - *Incubate:* Hire radicals who share core values with the group.
Improve	**Invest**
Purpose: Better quality and optimization *Integrated practices:* - *Incubate:* Add development of other people's creativity to the criteria for promotion. - *Imagine:* Use rapid prototyping processes to test the boundaries of a new idea or market. - *Invest:* Set stretch goals for the performance targets of projects.	*Purpose:* Fast profits *Integrated practices:* - *Improve:* Partner with a supplier that can help optimize your processes. - *Incubate:* Allocate significant resources to developing a community of practice. - *Imagine:* Advance more blue sky ideas through the portfolio process.

In each profile, the practices accommodate valuable qualities from other profiles, while remaining true to their purpose.

this exercise. Flip charts (or lots of paper), bold markers, and plenty of wall space is the best. (Look at the Jump-starting tool in Chapter Three for more ideas on logistics and facilitation.) You'll also need the creativity map the group developed in the exercise described in the "Setting Your Direction" section of this chapter.

Step 1. Look at the creativity map you developed that identifies the direction you want to go. Look at your number one priority and write the answers to the question "What do we need to get there?" As a group, generate ideas about what actions, changes, or practices will achieve your purposes. This should be a brain dump. Withhold judgment and simply generate as many ideas as possible. If you're not satisfied with the quantity or quality of your list, the Jump-starting tool offers trigger questions for creating divergent and convergent ideas (see Exhibit 3.1).

Step 2. As a group, select the idea you believe has the greatest potential as a solution. You might want to spend some time discussing this idea and what criteria it suggests that you are using, particularly on the basis of what profile it most represents.

Next, experiment with strengthening or modifying this idea by viewing it from the perspective of all four profiles. See Exhibit 7.3 for a list of trigger concepts that will help you relate your idea to the approaches or biases typical of each profile.

Write down all the ideas generated for each profile. Pick the best ideas generated by this step. You might want to select one idea from each of the profiles, or you might just select the three or four ideas that seem the most promising from the entire set of ideas. Write these "integrated ideas" somewhere the group can see them.

Step 3. Discuss the "integrated ideas" you have selected. Ask the following questions: How does each idea change what we are currently doing? How does this *enhance* our current practices? How does it *detract* from them?

With these answers in mind, decide how you are going to proceed. Create an action plan for how you are going to initiate

Exhibit 7.3. Trigger Concepts for Integrating Practices

View your idea from the perspective of each of the profiles by relating it to each list of trigger concepts. The goal is to see how you can strengthen or modify the idea by applying approaches or biases typical of each profile. For example, ask the group, "How do we make this idea more sustainable by communicating across networks?"

Incubate	Imagine
How do we make this idea *more sustainable?* *Think about . . .* <ul><li>Communicating across networks</li><li>Developing a cooperative community of practitioners</li><li>Nurturing shared values</li><li>Empowering people</li><li>Developing an inspiring workplace</li><li>Hiring talented people</li></ul>	How do we make this idea *newer?* *Think about . . .* <ul><li>Developing a vision of the future</li><li>Experimenting with radical ideas</li><li>Changing as we go along</li><li>Speculating emerging markets</li><li>Adopting new technology</li><li>Inventing breakthrough products and services</li></ul>
Improve	**Invest**
How do we make this idea *better?* *Think about . . .* <ul><li>Optimizing process</li><li>Cutting costs</li><li>Establishing rules and procedures</li><li>Defining roles</li><li>Improving existing products</li><li>Test models and prototypes</li></ul>	How do we make this idea *faster?* *Think about . . .* <ul><li>Increasing market share</li><li>Increasing revenues</li><li>Clarifying objectives</li><li>Extending a brand</li><li>Producing value for stakeholders</li><li>Recruiting partners</li></ul>

your integrated ideas. Assign tasks to the group members, taking into consideration basic questions like the following:

- *Who* is involved?
- *What* will happen?
- *Where* will this happen?
- *When* will this happen?
- *Why* are we doing this?
- *How* will this happen?

This activity might take part or all of a day. Afterward, give your team the time to consider, review, and revise this action plan, perhaps over two or three weeks. If needed, clarify the importance of the agreed-upon actions. Regularly have your team evaluate the impact of these actions and revise the list. Be aware that over time, the dominant profile is likely to change and require shifts in your action plan.

■ Developing the Creative Ability You Need

To complete any complex creative undertaking, whether as an individual or as the leader of a team, you must draw on all four profiles. This does not mean that you or your team are going to be equally good at all of them. Your success will depend upon your ability to identify and make the most of your existing strengths while you work to build up areas of weakness.

Some people learn faster than others, and some have greater range, but almost no one develops an ability without first determining that it is necessary and then identifying what needs to be done to develop it. This section addresses how you can develop needed competencies in your organization or group as well as in yourself.

Developing Appropriate Competencies and Practices in Your Group

Once you know your group's direction and have developed an action plan, you need the specific creative abilities to get where you want to go. Great leaders don't produce results themselves. Rather, they develop competencies and practices in their employees and colleagues so that many more people can produce results.

Creating a competency is often a much more important goal than any particular purpose. A competency can lead to the production of many new products and services that extend beyond the narrow aspirations of one purpose. Also, a competency is not susceptible to the fickle variations that the market produces. While your purposes may shift, your skills will last, providing your firm with intangible assets.[5]

Developing appropriate competencies and practices in your group begins with reviewing your creativity map and the action plan you have set. For each profile that your action plan incorporates, ask your group:

- What are the competencies and practices of this profile that are *required* to fulfill this action plan?
- What are the *current* competencies and practices of our group within this profile? (The assessment presented in Chapter Two can help you answer this question.)
- What *development activities* are required to fill the gap? Create a list of what needs to be done. If possible, break down these items to finer detail.

In the example in Exhibit 7.4, the group's action plan calls for creating inventive products. After assessing its strengths and weaknesses, the team has determined that it needs development activities for its managers and its culture, and that it also needs to change some general practices. Changing practices fundamental to the operation of the organization is how creativity moves from being a rare and discrete occurrence to an integral part of daily activities.

As a manager, you may need to look for imaginative ways of developing the competencies needed for your action plan. Few leaders have the luxury of starting fully funded with a winning strategy and hand-picked staff. Most often, you will need to work with your existing assets and constraints and gradually extend their boundaries. For example, if your team is strongly biased toward Improve practices, it may be difficult to get people to engage in more radical Imagine practices. However, some members

Exhibit 7.4. Developing Needed Team Competencies and Practices

The general purpose in this example is "To create more inventive products."

Incubate	Imagine
Required competencies and practices	*Required competencies and practices*
▪ A culture that supports creativity.	▪ More radical thinkers and risk takers.
Current competencies and practices	
▪ A culture that supports skill development.	*Current competencies and practices*
	▪ Leaders interested in developing creative thinkers.
Development activities required	
▪ Regular retreats to develop shared vision and values, including follow-up activities.	*Development activities required*
	▪ Changing hiring and promotion practices.
Improve	**Invest**
Required competencies and practices	*Required competencies and practices*
▪ Operating directors develop rapid prototyping skills	▪ Capital allocation team that picks winning projects, products, and ventures.
Current competencies and practices	
▪ Operating directors have skills for efficient and quality-based manufacturing.	*Current competencies and practices*
	▪ Capital allocation team that follows the industry trends.
Development activities required	
▪ Train operating directors in new manufacturing techniques and rotate their assignments.	*Development activities required*
	▪ Changing the way the capital allocation team funds initiatives.

of the team may be favorably biased toward Imagine practices. You might give those people Imagine-type projects or spin them off as a separate subteam. You could also complement your group's strengths by partnering with another team that demonstrates greater competencies in Imagine-style creativity. To get the most from your team, you might want to consider your team members' preferred work conditions and interaction style. Exhibit 7.5 lists the workplace preferences that are common for each profile.

Developing Yourself

As noted, projects and initiatives are likely to change as they move through from conception to commercialization. A different creative approach will be required to achieve the desired outcomes in each phase.

There are two basic approaches you can take to fulfilling roles that make different creativity demands. The first is to adjust your roles to reflect your strengths. That can mean supporting yourself with people whose creativity strengths complement your own. The second approach is to work to acquire new skills in the profiles where you are weakest.

Often it is wise to focus on building on your creativity strengths. You are most likely to produce value to a group by doing what you do best. One way of making the most of your creative abilities is to make a list of the things you do at work, particularly those you identify with creativity. Giving an honest look at these competencies and practices, ask yourself the following questions:

- Where am I incompetent? (Things you don't do well.)
- Where am I competent? (Things you do to an acceptable level.)
- Where am I masterful? (Things you do very well.)
- Where am I unique? (Things you do better than anyone you know.)

Typically, it is hardest to answer the first and last questions. Talk with your friends and colleagues to get additional perspectives on your abilities. Also pay attention to the circumstances that influence your creativity. Are you a morning creator? Do you

Exhibit 7.5. Working with People Who Favor Each Profile

Use these lists of preferences to help you consider your team members'
preferred work conditions and interaction style.

Incubate	Imagine
Ideal Working Conditions	*Ideal Working Conditions*
■ Family atmosphere	■ Stimulating
■ Collaborative work	■ Flexible
■ Shared values and vision	■ Informal
■ Calm and therapeutic work space	■ Free from everyday constraints
■ Time to reflect	■ Stimulating new people, projects, and information
■ Friendly coworkers	■ Independent
■ Integrated personal and professional goals	■ Diverse
■ Agreed approaches for resolving conflicts	*How to Work with Imagine People*
■ Limits on personal demands	■ Play with them
	■ Share their enthusiasm and vision
How to Work with Incubate People	■ Be stimulating
■ Be informal	■ Bring new ideas to talk about
■ Build rapport and trust	■ Avoid details
■ Think of others first	■ Help them put their ideas into action
■ Show your emotions and look for theirs	■ Recognize their accomplishments
■ Listen	
■ Ask how they feel about an idea	
■ Offer your assistance and support	

Improve	Invest
Ideal Working Conditions	*Ideal Working Conditions*
■ Clear roles and responsibilities	■ Competitive
■ Stability	■ Work has big, direct impact
■ Clear objectives, operating processes, and standards	■ Fast moving
■ Ordered and structured work environment	■ Deal making
■ Respect for superiors	■ Image enhancing
■ Adequate time to complete complex projects correctly	■ With quantifiable results
■ Access to technology, tools, and data	■ With winners
	■ Where success is rewarded
How to Work with Improve People	■ High energy
■ Present the facts methodically	*How to Work with Invest People*
■ Be specific	■ Focus on achieving their goals
■ Show the data and details	■ Stick to business
■ Ask for their suggestions	■ Show them the money
■ Create a project plan and time-line, and show the steps	■ Get to the point
■ Be punctual	■ Let them own their work
■ Make contingency plans	■ Be decisive
■ Reduce the risk	■ Just the facts
■ Agree to check off with superiors	■ Provide a few clear and logical choices
■ Fit ideas within existing operating plans	■ Focus disagreements on the facts and away from personalities

create better when there is music playing? Do you find that you create better when in a group? What types of people elicit your best creativity? Considering these questions may help you identify additional facets of your personal abilities. Once you have identified your creativity strengths and weaknesses, you can arrange them as shown in Figure 7.1.

A picture like this one will help you figure out how to take action to capitalize on your strengths. Ask yourself the following questions:

- How do my strengths and weaknesses correspond with the creativity map? What does this picture tell me about my own creativity profile?
- How can I reduce my duties in the areas where I am incompetent or merely competent? (For example, delegate, train others, take on new job responsibilities.)
- How can I develop other people so they can take a greater role in areas where I am competent and masterful? (Mentor others, partner with them, hire people who can share responsibility in these areas.)
- How can I arrange my responsibilities so I employ more of my unique competencies? (Change my priorities, change the way I do my job, take on new initiatives, move to a new employer.)

Although you can play to your strengths by focusing on situations where your existing creative abilities will result in success, you can decide to address your weaknesses instead. One way to do so is by getting into situations where you are destined to make mistakes so that you will learn from them. It's also useful to surround yourself with people who have the type of skills you wish to develop. The more diverse your community of practice, the more likely you are to develop new skills.

Exhibit 7.6 shows some activities and questions that you can try in each profile. You can discover your own creative pref-

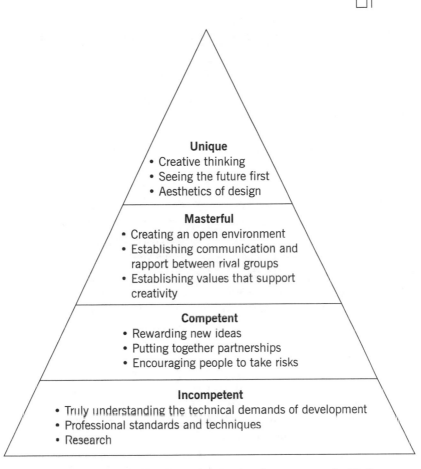

Unique
- Creative thinking
- Seeing the future first
- Aesthetics of design

Masterful
- Creating an open environment
- Establishing communication and rapport between rival groups
- Establishing values that support creativity

Competent
- Rewarding new ideas
- Putting together partnerships
- Encouraging people to take risks

Incompetent
- Truly understanding the technical demands of development
- Professional standards and techniques
- Research

In this example, this person's strongest competencies correspond with the Imagine profile and the weakest competencies are in the Improve profile.

Figure 7.1. Example of Analyzing Personal Competencies

erences by experimenting. Take on new projects and work on them in new ways with new people. Keep an idea log to document your ideas and reactions. Use this idea log to start a dialogue with yourself about how you are creating, what feels right, and what results you produce.

Adjust your strategy according to your own honest assessment of yourself. For those who can effectively create in several profiles, working on a series of diverse projects or on a few projects

Exhibit 7.6. Actions to Try and Questions to Ask in Developing Your Creativity

Incubate	Imagine
Useful Maneuvers	*Useful Maneuvers*
▪ Collaborate with others who share your values.	▪ Change where you work—and how, when, with whom, and most important, why.
▪ Enjoy the act of creating as a form of personal therapy.	▪ Challenge assumptions, conventions, and most of all, authority.
▪ Look for ways in which your personal creative and spiritual life can fit into your professional one.	▪ See your future as a discontinuous and incongruous adventure.
▪ Network and join groups that share your creative interests.	▪ Develop a deep sense of destiny about your work.
▪ Find a mentor to help you learn and develop as a creative person. Coach others.	▪ Treat your job as an assortment of radically different experiments.
▪ Create a work space that inspires your creativity.	▪ Schedule slack time into your planner.
	▪ Fall in love with your ideas but be willing to move on when they don't work out.
Potential Dangers	
▪ "Group think"	*Potential Dangers*
▪ Complacent atmosphere	▪ Spinning out into chaos
▪ Sidestepping productive conflict	▪ Thinking "Anything goes"
	▪ Confusing creative expression with creative outcomes
Questions to Ask Yourself	
▪ Are we creating community?	*Questions to Ask Yourself*
▪ Are we creating knowledge?	▪ Is this idea really new?
	▪ Will this idea create growth?

Improve	Invest
Useful Maneuvers	*Useful Maneuvers*
▪ Break large projects down into a series of smaller ones.	▪ Be the CEO of yourself by setting important goals and working toward big rewards.
▪ Add technology and systems to your creative toolkit.	▪ Enlist motivated and capable partners.
▪ Study your craft deeply.	▪ Invest in ideas that have a clear road to riches.
▪ Gather data and analyze what works and what doesn't.	▪ Make the most of trial and error by starting lots of projects and completing only the few that continue to show merit.
▪ Create an enabling method to support your creative process.	
▪ Align yourself with professionals whose roles and responsibilities complement and improve your own.	▪ Decide what you are and are not going to work on. Be decisive.
▪ Make your existing job better.	▪ Set measurable goals that can be achieved quickly.
Potential Dangers	▪ Motivate yourself and energize others through friendly contests.
▪ Bureaucracy	*Potential Dangers*
▪ Overreliance on scientific thinking	▪ Competing over everything
▪ Excessive data gathering and analysis	▪ Funding only those projects with an immediate pay-out
	▪ The win-or-lose mentality
Questions to Ask Yourself	*Questions to Ask Yourself*
▪ Is this product or process done well?	▪ Is this really fast enough?
▪ Is this process optimized?	▪ Is this worth something?

in multiple ways makes sense. For those who are predisposed to create within a single profile, working in a similar role on multiple projects is better. Often, areas where we are not unique are areas where others around us are stronger. By doing what we do best, we may help others do their best as well. Remember that you are an individual within a business. To be creative requires that you are mindful of how your own profile and abilities interrelate with others, your situation, and your purpose.

Putting Creativity to Work

Putting your own creativity to work can and should be done on both a personal and organizational level. As an individual, you can use this book to help you reflect on your aspirations and development. Consider your relationship with all of the profiles, particularly your current state and future goals. However, your personal creativity is only the beginning. Your greater impact will be determined by your ability to encourage others to be creators and to move purposefully as a group toward shared goals.

In the end, your effectiveness as a leader will be determined by your ability to make your organization, your community, and yourself better and new. Put your creativity to work and you will follow a path to future value and new horizons.

CHAPTER SUMMARY

The real art of creativity management and leadership is blending the four profiles, because most work situations have a blend of purposes. No matter what your level of responsibility, you can use the entire creativity map to guide, manage, and integrate creativity practices within your organization, division, department, or team.

First you need to set your direction, accounting for the inherent tensions that exist between profiles. This tension is healthy. You will want to consider the purposes for your entire organization, the business unit within which your own group operates, and the subgroups that are part of your group. Then consider your own group's current biases and tendencies and the purposes it needs to pursue in each profile. By prioritizing this list, your group can establish a sense of direction.

Second, you need to create an action plan that allows you to integrate creativity practices appropriate to your situation and that helps you overcome the three principal barriers you're likely to encounter: incompatible purposes and practices, negative zones, and multiple purposes and practices. The most effective way to address the issue of multiple purposes and practices is through integration. To integrate, you need to accommodate and retain the qualities of another profile within your dominant profile by considering your potential actions or ideas from the perspective of each of the other profiles.

Finally, you will want to develop creative ability in your team and in yourself by identifying and making the most of existing strengths while building up areas of weakness. Use your action plan to determine the required and current competencies and practices of your group. Consider the development activities required to fill the gap and how you can make the most of your team members' preferences. You will also want to consider your own preferences and abilities and how you might want to shift your personal work responsibilities to grow or fit these tendencies.

Through a review of your personal and organizational creativity profiles and aspirations, you will be better able to serve your organization by encouraging creativity in yourself and others. Together you can move purposefully toward future value.

Notes

Chapter One

1. Our model is based on the Competing Values Framework (CVF), which has been used to explain organizational effectiveness, culture, life cycles, and change, as well as leadership style. For more information on the origins of this model, see Robert E. Quinn and John Rohrbaugh, "A Competing Values Approach to Organizational Effectiveness," *Public Productivity Review* 5, no. 2 (1981): 122–140; and Robert E. Quinn, "Applying the Competing Values Approach to Leadership: Toward an Integrative Framework," in *Leaders and Managers: International Perspectives on Managerial Behavior and Leadership,* edited by James G. Hunt, Dian-Marie Hosking, Chester A. Schriesheim, and Rosemary Stewart (New York: Pergamon Press, 1984), pp. 10–27.
2. This story is based on Richard Schickel, "Ruler of the Magic Kingdom: Walt Disney," *Time* 152, no. 23 (December 7, 1998): 124–127.
3. This story is based on John Greenwald, "Master of the Mainframe: Thomas Watson, Jr.," *Time* 152, no. 23 (December 7, 1998): 170–172.
4. This story is based on Jacques Pepin, "Burger Meister: Ray Kroc," *Time* 152, no. 23 (December 7, 1998): 176–178.

5. This story is based on Susan Cheever, "The Healer: Bill W.," *Time* 153, no. 23 (June 14, 1999): 201–204.

Chapter Two

1. The following story is based on Leslie Goff, "1972: Xerox Parc and the Alto," *Computer World/Cable News Network* (July 8, 1999), retrieved January 9, 2002, from http://www.cnn.com/TECH/computing/9907/08/1972.idg/. It also uses Xerox Corporation, "PARC's Legacy," retrieved January 9, 2002, from http://www.parc.xerox.com/hist-1st.html.
2. These forms of value are often called *value propositions* in the business press.

Chapter Three

1. Clayton M. Christensen, *The Innovator's Dilemma: When New Technologies Cause Great Firms to Fail* (Boston: Harvard Business School Press, 1997).
2. Ronald S. Jonash and Tom Sommerlatte, *The Innovation Premium: How Next Generation Companies Are Achieving Peak Performance and Profitability* (Cambridge, MA: Perseus, 1999).
3. Jack Smith, "The Deep Dive: One Company's Secret Weapon for Innovation," *Nightline with Ted Koppel* (ABC News Videos, July 13, 1999), Television program. Available from ABC News Store, 800–505–6139, Item # N990713.
4. This story is based on Paul J. Lim, "Fluke Is Rebounding: Firm Changes Product Mix with Success," *Seattle Times* (March 13, 1995): C1; and Eric Matson, "Here, Innovation Is No Fluke," *Fast Company* (August-September 1997): 42–44.
5. Robert E. Quinn, *Deep Change: Discovering the Leader Within* (San Francisco: Jossey-Bass, 1996).
6. Mihaly Csikszentmihalyi, *Flow: The Psychology of Optimal Experience* (New York: Harper Perennial, 1990).
7. John Grossman, "Jump Start Your Business," *Inc.* 19, no. 6 (May 1, 1997): 36–54.

8. Kathleen M. Eisenhardt, Jean L. Kahwajy, and L. J. Bourgeois III, "How Management Teams Can Have a Good Fight," *Harvard Business Review* 75, no. 4 (1997): 77–85.
9. Smith, "The Deep Dive."
10. "Reuters Group PLC Company Profile," retrieved February 22, 2001, from Hoover's Online Database (http://www.hoovers.com).
11. Dorothy Leonard-Barton, "Core Capabilities and Core Rigidities: A Paradox in Managing New Product Development," in *Managing Strategic Innovation and Change,* edited by Michael L. Tushman and Philip Anderson (New York: Oxford University Press, 1997), pp. 255–270; C. K. Prahalad and Gary Hamel, "The Core Competence of the Corporation," *Harvard Business Review* 68, no. 3 (1990): 79–91.
12. Norman R. F. Maier, "Assets and Liabilities in Group Problem Solving: The Need for an Integrative Function," *Psychological Review* 74 (1967): 239–249.
13. Jim Channon, interview by Katherine Lawrence and Kimberly Hannon Parrott, May 2, 2001. For more information about Arcturus, visit http://www.arcturus.org/.

Chapter Four

1. This story is based on "eBay Inc. Company Profile," retrieved October 22, 2001, from Hoover's Online Database (http://www.hoovers.com/); Brian Caulfield, "Small Fees, Big Volume Are Keys for Auctioneer," *Internet World* (March 9, 1998), retrieved February 22, 2001, from Lexis-Nexis database; and visits to the eBay Web site during October 2001 (http://www.ebay.com/).
2. Ronald S. Burt, *Structural Holes: The Social Structure of Competition* (Cambridge, MA: Harvard University Press, 1992).
3. Carl Shapiro and Hal R. Varian, *Information Rules: A Strategic Guide to the Network Economy* (Boston: Harvard Business School Press, 1999).
4. Brian Uzzi, "Social Structure and Competition in Interfirm Networks: The Paradox of Embeddedness," *Administrative Science Quarterly* 42 (1997): 35–67.

5. Robert G. Cooper, Scott J. Edgett, and Elko J. Kleinschmidt, *Portfolio Management for New Products* (Reading, MA: Addison-Wesley, 1998); and Robert G. Cooper, Scott J. Edgett, and Elko J. Kleinschmidt, "New Problems, New Solutions: Making Portfolio Management More Effective," *Research-Technology Management* (March-April 2000): 18–33.

6. Cooper, Edgett, and Kleinschmidt, "New Problems, New Solutions."

7. Cooper, Edgett, and Kleinschmidt, "New Problems, New Solutions"; Cooper, Edgett, and Kleinschmidt, *Portfolio Management for New Products.*

8. Robert G. Cooper, "From Experience: The Invisible Success Factors in Product Innovation," *Journal of Product Innovation Management* 16 (1999): 115–133.

9. Barry M. Staw and Jerry Ross, "Understanding Behavior in Escalation Situations," *Science* 246 (October 13, 1989): 216–220.

10. Steven C. Wheelwright and Kim B. Clark, "Creating Project Plans to Focus Product Development," *Harvard Business Review* (March-April 1992): 70–82; and Cooper, "From Experience."

11. This story is based on Eric Matson, "He Turns Ideas into Companies— at Net Speed," *Fast Company* (December-January 1996): 34–36; Joseph Nocera, "Why Is He Still Smiling?" *Fortune* (March 2001), retrieved July 18, 2001, from Business 2.0 Web site, http://www.busiss2.com/articles/mag/print/0,1643,9503,00.html; Charles Platt, "What's the Big Idea?" *Wired* (September 1999), retrieved July 18, 2001, from Wired Web site (http://www.wired.com/); and Jerry Useem, "The Start-up Factory," *Inc.* (February 1997), retrieved July 18, 2001, from Inc. Online, http://mothra.inc.com/incmagazine/archives/02970401.html.

12. Nocera, "Why Is He Still Smiling?"

13. Lawsuit information comes from Karen Kaplan, "Investors Want Idealab Liquidated," *Los Angeles Times* (January 19, 2002): section 3, page 1; and Cheryl Meyer, "Investors: Idealab Broke Securities Law," *Daily Deal* Web edition (March 1, 2002), retrieved April 17, 2002, from the Daily Deal Web site (http://www.thedeal.com/).

14. Useem, "The Start-up Factory"; and Morten T. Hansen, Henry W. Chesbrough, Nitin Nohria, and Donald N. Sull, "Networked Incubators: Hothouses of the New Economy," *Harvard Business Review* (September-October 2000): 74–83.

15. Platt, "What's the Big Idea?"
16. Andrew Hargadon and Robert I. Sutton, "Building an Innovation Factory," *Harvard Business Review* (May-June 2000): 157–166.
17. Michael D. Cohen, James G. March, and Johan P. Olsen, "A Garbage Can Model of Organizational Choice," *Administrative Science Quarterly* 17 (1972): 1–25.
18. For more ideas, see Cooper, Edgett, and Kleinschmidt, "New Problems, New Solutions"; and Cooper, Edgett, and Kleinschmidt, *Portfolio Management for New Products.*

Chapter Five

1. The observations about modular systems in this section are based primarily on Carliss Y. Baldwin and Kim B. Clark, "Managing in an Age of Modularity," *Harvard Business Review* (September-October 1997): 84–93; and Marc H. Meyer and Robert Seliger, "Product Platforms in Software Development," *Sloan Management Review* 40, no. 1 (1998): 61–74.
2. Dorothy Leonard-Barton, H. Kent Bowen, Kim B. Clark, Charles A. Holloway, and Steven C. Wheelwright, "How to Integrate Work *and* Deepen Expertise," *Harvard Business Review* (September-October 1994): 121–130; see pp. 124, 125.
3. Jack Smith, "The Deep Dive: One Company's Secret Weapon for Innovation," *Nightline with Ted Koppel* (ABC News Videos, July 13, 1999), Television program.
4. This story is based on conversations with Richard Sheridan and James Goebel, interview by Katherine Lawrence, November 6, 2001. For further information about the implementation of Extreme Programming, Sheridan and Goebel can be reached at http://www.Menlolnnovations.com/. Additional details in this story come from Jeff Bennett, "Michigan Is Caught in Technology Industry's Merger Mania," *Detroit Free Press* (September 26, 2000); and Kent Beck, *Extreme Programming Explained: Embrace Change* (Boston: Addison-Wesley, 2000).
5. Beck, *Extreme Programming Explained.*
6. Beck, *Extreme Programming Explained,* p. 29.
7. Lee Fleming and Olav Sorenson, "The Dangers of Modularity," *Harvard Business Review* (September, 2001): 2–3.

8. Marco Iansiti and Alan MacCormack, "Developing Products on Internet Time," *Harvard Business Review* (September-October 1997): 108–117.

9. Beck, *Extreme Programming Explained.*

10. Rebecca M. Henderson and Kim B. Clark, "Architectural Innovation: The Reconfiguration of Existing Product Technologies and the Failure of Established Firms," *Administrative Science Quarterly* 35 (1990): 9–30.

11. Henderson and Clark, "Architectural Innovation."

12. John Seely Brown, "Seeing Differently: A Role for Pioneering Research," *Research-Technology Management* (May-June 1998): 24–33.

13. Michael Schrage, *Serious Play: How the World's Best Companies Simulate to Innovate* (Boston: Harvard Business School Press, 2000).

14. Baldwin and Clark, "Managing in an Age of Modularity."

15. This story and the subsequent analysis are based on Durward K. Sobek II, Jeffrey K. Liker, and Allen C. Ward, "Another Look at How Toyota Integrates Product Development," *Harvard Business Review* (July-August 1998): 36–48; and "Toyota Motor Corporation Company Profile," retrieved January 20, 2002, from Hoover's Online Database (http://www.hoovers.com/).

16. Ralph Katz and Thomas J. Allen, "Organizational Issues in the Introduction of New Technologies," in *The Human Side of Managing Technological Innovation,* edited by Ralph Katz (New York: Oxford University Press, 1997), pp. 384–397.

17. Viola Spolin, *Improvisation for the Theater* (Evanston, IL: Northwestern University Press, 1983).

18. Min Basadur, "Managing Creativity: A Japanese Model," *Academy of Management Executive* 6, no. 2 (1992): 29–42.

19. Christopher Meyer, "A Six-Step Framework for Becoming a Fast-Cycle-Time Competitor," in *The Human Side of Managing Technological Innovation,* pp. 487–499.

20. Kathleen M. Eisenhardt and Donald N. Sull, "Strategy as Simple Rules," *Harvard Business Review* (January 2001): 107–116.

21. Sobek, Liker, and Ward, "Another Look at How Toyota Integrates Product Development."

22. For a detailed guide to this process, see Dave Ulrich, Steve Kerr, and Ron Ashkenas, *The GE Work-Out* (New York: McGraw-Hill, 2002).

Chapter Six

1. This story and the following discussion are based on Norman P. Findley, "Entrepreneurship in the Organization: Comments from Arthur Blank, President and Chief Operating Officer of The Home Depot," *Babson Entrepreneurial Review* 12, no. 1 (March 1997): 16–18; and Bernie Marcus and Arthur Blank, *Built From Scratch: How a Couple of Regular Guys Grew The Home Depot from Nothing to $30 Billion* (New York: Random House, 1999).
2. Marcus and Blank, *Built From Scratch,* p. 279.
3. Marcus and Blank, *Built From Scratch,* p. 107.
4. Findley, "Entrepreneurship in the Organization," p. 16.
5. Dorothy Leonard, *Wellsprings of Knowledge: Building and Sustaining the Sources of Innovation* (Boston: Harvard Business School Press, 1995), p. 62.
6. Jerry Hirshberg, *The Creative Priority: Putting Innovation to Work in Your Business* (New York: HarperBusiness, 1998), p. 34.
7. Jon R. Katzenbach and Douglas K. Smith, *The Wisdom of Teams: Creating the High-Performance Organization* (New York: HarperBusiness, 1993), p. 48.
8. Katzenbach and Smith, *The Wisdom of Teams,* p. 46.
9. Robert E. Quinn and Gretchen M. Spreitzer, "The Road to Empowerment: Seven Questions Every Leader Should Consider," *Organizational Dynamics* 26, no. 2 (1997): 37–49.
10. The observations in the two sentences preceding this note are from Dvora Yanow, "Translating Local Knowledge at Organizational Peripheries" (paper presented at the Interdisciplinary Committee on Organizational Studies, Ann Arbor, MI, March 30, 2001).
11. J. Richard Hackman and Greg R. Oldham, *Work Redesign* (Reading, MA: Addison-Wesley, 1980).
12. Min Basadur, "Managing Creativity: A Japanese Model," *Academy of Management Executive* 6, no. 2 (1992): 29–42.
13. Tom Peters, *The Tom Peters Seminar: Crazy Times Call for Crazy Organizations* (New York: Vintage Books, 1994).
14. Charles Fishman, "Whole Foods Is All Teams," *Fast Company* (April–May 1996): 102–111.
15. Patagonia, "Defining Quality: A Brief Description of How We Got Here," Corporate brochure (Fall 1998), retrieved January 16, 2002

from the Patagonia "Press Room" Web site: http://www.patagonia.com/culture/press_room.shtml.

16. John E. Tropman, *The Compensation Solution: How to Develop an Employee-Driven Rewards System* (San Francisco: Jossey-Bass, 2001).

17. This story is based on Charles Fishman, "Sabbaticals Are Serious Business," *Fast Company* (October-November 1996): 44–46; and Gordon MacKenzie, *Orbiting the Giant Hairball: A Corporate Fool's Guide to Surviving with Grace* (New York: Viking, 1998).

18. MacKenzie, *Orbiting the Giant Hairball,* p. 143.

19. MacKenzie, *Orbiting the Giant Hairball,* p. 149.

20. Tony Hiss, *The Experience of Place* (New York: Viking, 1990).

21. Michael Brill of the Buffalo Organization for Social and Technological Innovation, cited in Hiss, *The Experience of Place,* pp. 17–18.

22. These consulting firms can be found on the Web at http://www.ideo.com/, http://www.eurekaranch.com/, and http://www.knowherestore.com/.

23. Tom Kelley, *The Art of Innovation: Lessons in Creativity from IDEO, America's Leading Design Firm* (New York: Doubleday, 2001), p. 121.

24. Malcolm Gladwell, "Designs for Working," *New Yorker* (December 11, 2000): 60–70.

25. Thomas J. Allen, "Communication Networks in R&D Laboratories," in *The Human Side of Managing Technological Innovation,* edited by Ralph Katz (New York: Oxford University Press, 1997), pp. 320–330.

26. MacKenzie, *Orbiting the Giant Hairball.*

27. Kimberly D. Elsbach, "In Search of Mindless Work: Thoughts on Job Design and the Rhythm of Managerial Thinking," (paper presented at the Academy of Management Conference, Washington, DC, August 7, 2001).

28. Etienne Wenger, "Communities of Practice and Social Learning Systems," *Organization* 7, no. 2 (2000): 225–246.

29. John Van Maanen and Stephen R. Barley, "Occupational Communities: Culture and Control in Organizations," in *Research in Organizational Behavior,* Vol. 6, edited by Barry M. Staw and Larry L. Cummings (Greenwich, CT: JAI Press, 1984), pp. 287–365; John Seely Brown and Paul Duguid, "Organizational Learning and Communities-of-Practice: Toward a Unified View of Working, Learning, and Innovation," in *Orga-*

nizational Learning, edited by Michael D. Cohen and Lee S. Sproull (Thousand Oaks, CA: Sage, 1996), pp. 58–82; and Ikujiro Nonaka, "A Dynamic Theory of Organizational Knowledge Creation," *Organization Science* 5, no. 1 (1994): 14–37.

30. Richard B. Sheridan, "Using a Breakthrough Development Process to go from Legacy to Internet: Transforming Interface Systems to an Internet Business," (paper presented at the New Product Development Forum, Product Development and Management Association, Ann Arbor, MI, December 12, 2000).

31. For a comprehensive look at the value of networking and social capital, see Wayne Baker, *Achieving Success Through Social Capital: Tapping the Hidden Resources in Your Personal and Business Networks* (San Francisco: Jossey-Bass, 2000).

32. The culture of a group is the set of shared fundamental assumptions that shape the way that members think and function in that setting. See Joanne Martin, *Organizational Culture: Mapping the Terrain* (Thousand Oaks, CA: Sage, 2002); and Edgar H. Schein, *Organizational Culture and Leadership,* 2nd ed. (San Francisco: Jossey-Bass, 1992).

33. Harrison M. Trice and Janice M. Beyer, *The Cultures of Work Organizations* (Upper Saddle River, NJ: Prentice Hall, 1993).

34. John Van Maanen and Gideon Kunda, "'Real Feelings': Emotional Expression and Organizational Culture," in *Research in Organizational Behavior,* Vol. 11, edited by Larry L. Cummings and Barry M. Staw (Greenwich, CT: JAI Press, 1989), pp. 43–103.

Chapter Seven

1. "Corning Incorporated Company Profile," retrieved October 21, 2001, from Hoover's Online Database (http://www.hoovers.com/).

2. Charles Fishman, "Creative Tension," *Fast Company* (November 2000): 358–388.

3. Dorothy Leonard-Barton, "Core Capabilities and Core Rigidities: A Paradox in Managing New Product Development," in *Managing Strategic Innovation and Change,* edited by Michael L. Tushman and Philip Anderson (New York: Oxford University Press, 1997), pp. 255–270.

4. John A. Boquist, Todd T. Milbourn, and Anjan V. Thakor, *The Value Sphere: Secrets of Creating and Retaining Shareholder Wealth* (Bloomington, IN: Value Integration Associates, 2000).

5. Richard E. S. Boulton, Barry D. Libert, and Steve M. Samek, *Cracking the Value Code: How Successful Businesses Are Creating Wealth in the New Economy* (New York: HarperCollins, 2000).

Additional Resources and Readings

Online Assessment

The *Creativity at Work* Web site, http://www.creativity-at-work.com/.

This Web site provides an on-line version of the assessment in Chapter Two of this book. In addition, it offers resources not included in the book, such as links to helpful sources of information, exemplary firms, creativity specialists, and other services.

Purposes

B. Joseph Pine II and James H. Gilmore, *The Experience Economy: Work Is Theatre and Every Business a Stage* (Boston: Harvard Business School Press, 1999).

This book proposes that the ultimate value a company offers is the "theatrical" experience that accompanies any product or service. Because customers are willing to pay extra for memorable, distinctive, or customized experiences, companies should consider these experiences to be an additional outlet for creating value.

Michael Treacy and Fred Wiersema, "Customer Intimacy and Other Value Disciplines," *Harvard Business Review* (January-February, 1993), reprint number 93107.

This article offers a good overview of the importance of selecting practices to achieve appropriate forms of value. Examples illustrate three "value disciplines" and the practices that support these outcomes.

Personal Creativity

James M. Higgins, *101 Creative Problem Solving Techniques: The Handbook of New Ideas for Business* (Winter Park, FL: New Management, 1994).

This book is a brilliantly integrated collection of useful creativity tools and techniques. It indexes when to use what tools and gives detailed explanations of how to facilitate them.

Gordon MacKenzie, *Orbiting the Giant Hairball: A Corporate Fool's Guide to Surviving with Grace* (New York: Viking, 1998).

An autobiography of sorts, this book offers a collection of stories, parables, and insights on the nature of personal creativity within organizational settings. A delightful and inspiring read.

Roger Von Oech, *A Whack on the Side of the Head* (New York: Warner Books, 1998).

One of the best how-to books around. Von Oech provides a simple method for being creative in different situations.

Jump-Starting

Doug Hall, *Jump Start Your Brain* (New York: Warner Books, 1996).

Hall, an expert at running jump-starting retreats, suggests how to use groups of "ordinary" people—rather than specialized experts or designers—in the development of new products and services.

Tom Kelley with Jonathan Littman, *The Art of Innovation: Lessons in Creativity from IDEO, America's Leading Design Firm* (New York: Currency/Doubleday, 2001).

IDEO may well be the premiere new product design firm in the world. This book lays out how the company's management and employees run brainstorming sessions, work in groups, create prototypes, design their work environment, and encourage innovation. The video about IDEO's brainstorming process is also worthwhile: Jack Smith, "The Deep Dive: One Company's Secret Weapon for Innovation," *Nightline with Ted Koppel* (ABC News Videos, July 13, 1999), Television program. Available from ABC News Store, 800–505–6139, Item # N990713.

Forecasting

Gary Hamel and C. K. Prahalad, *Competing for the Future* (Boston: Harvard Business School Press, 1994).

This book proposes that the future belongs to those firms that can get there first. It provides suggestions on how companies can develop unique core competencies that will allow them to shape the future rather than following it.

Peter Schwartz, *The Art of the Long View: Planning for the Future in an Uncertain World* (New York: Doubleday, 1996).

Futurist Schwartz introduces a revolutionary approach to developing strategic foresight. This book provides useful methods (such as scenario planning) for envisioning the future first.

Partnering

Yves Doz and Gary Hamel, *Alliance Advantage: The Art of Creating Value Through Partnering* (Boston: Harvard Business School Press, 1998).

This book suggests that globalization and mergers have made it almost impossible for firms to complete without strong allies. It gives practical advice on how to evaluate, create, and maintain alliances of all types.

Philip Evans and Thomas Wurster, *Blown to Bits: How the New Economics of Information Transforms Strategy* (Boston: Harvard Business School Press, 2000).

This book spells out how the Internet and other technologies change the competitive landscape of markets where large incumbent firms usually enjoy the competitive advantages of greater reach. These authors suggest new ways of using the Internet to support partnering and offer strategies for firms of all sizes to maneuver effectively in this new space.

Portfolios

Robert G. Cooper, Scott J. Edgett, and Elko J. Kleinschmidt, *Portfolio Management for New Products* (Reading, MA: Addison-Wesley, 1998).

This is a must-have book for anyone who is serious about establishing an integrated process for launching and funding initiatives with a portfolio method. Learn about how investors and financial departments evaluate new ideas and gain the upper hand in getting your projects funded.

W. Chan Kim and Renée Mauborgne, "Knowing a Winning Business Idea When You See One," *Harvard Business Review* (September-October 2000), reprint number 00510.

This article provides some key insights into why certain products and services are likely to succeed in the marketplace. It outlines a straightforward framework for picking winners.

Modular Design and Development

Kent Beck, *Extreme Programming Explained: Embrace Change* (Reading, MA: Addison-Wesley, 2000).

This book offers the original, definitive description of "Extreme Programming," the software version of modular design and development. Other books in this series are also helpful.

Michael Schrage, *Serious Play: How the World's Best Companies Simulate to Innovate* (Boston: Harvard Business School Press, 2000).

Schrage, a leading business technology journalist, reviews how models, prototypes, and simulations are blurring the boundary between designing a new product and manufacturing it. Learn about the emerging technologies and methodologies that enable rapid prototyping and platform innovation.

Preston Smith and Donald Reinertsen, *Developing Products in Half the Time* (New York: Wiley, 1997).

This book combines methods for effective resource use with techniques for accelerating product development. It describes the applications and limitations of numerous practical tools for reducing cycle time.

Process Improvement Systems

Jean Philippe Deschamps and P. Ranganath Mayak, *Product Juggernauts: How Companies Mobilize to Generate a Stream of Market Winners* (Boston: Harvard Business School Press, 1995).

This book looks at the wide array of key components that factor into the ongoing processes of making a product a winner. It integrates product design, manufacturing, sales, and customer service into a system to refine, adapt, and improve existing products and to create new ones. It includes material on Toyota as well.

Phillip H. Francis, *Product Creation: The Heart of the Enterprise from Engineering to E-Commerce* (New York: Free Press, 2000).

Francis asserts that all functions in the company must work as a team to create new products. He outlines all the processes—and potential difficulties—of creating new products so that nonengineers can understand and support product development effectively.

Durward K. Sobek II, Jeffrey K. Liker, and Allen C. Ward, "Another Look at How Toyota Integrates Product Development," *Harvard Business Review* (July-August, 1998), reprint number 98409.

This article offers a very clear breakdown of the ways that Toyota structures and integrates the product development process through carefully balanced mechanisms.

Talent Scouting

Jon R. Katzenbach and Douglas K. Smith, *The Wisdom of Teams: Creating the High-Performance Organization* (New York: HarperBusiness, 1993).

This highly readable book is filled with guidelines and examples for developing high-performance teams that share values and goals. In particular, the authors encourage building community, mutual accountability, and developing capabilities on the job.

Dorothy Leonard, *Wellsprings of Knowledge: Building and Sustaining the Sources of Innovation* (Boston: Harvard Business School Press, 1995).

Harvard Business School professor Leonard explores how the "knowledge assets" of a firm lead to the creation of new products. This book has particularly helpful chapters on identifying individual "signature skills" and combining people into effective, diverse combinations that can build core capabilities.

Jeffrey Pfeffer and Robert I. Sutton, *The Knowing-Doing Gap* (Boston: Harvard Business School Press, 2000).

Stanford professors Pfeffer and Sutton point out that businesses spend too much time studying how to gather knowledge instead of using it. Based on years of research, this book provides useful recommendations on how to help an organization develop ability through a culture that supports hands-on experimentation and distributed decision making in a cooperative, team-minded atmosphere.

Idea Spaces

Franklin Becker and Fritz Steele, *Workplace by Design: Mapping the High-Performance Workscape* (San Francisco: Jossey-Bass, 1995).

This book looks at how to create workspaces that can encourage creativity. It covers issues related to workflow, status and identity, flexibility, teams, health factors, and virtual workers.

Georg von Krosh, Kazuo Ichijo, and Ikujiro Nonaka, *Enabling Knowledge Creation: How to Unlock the Mystery of Tacit Knowledge and Release the Power of Innovation* (Oxford, UK: Oxford University Press, 2000).

This book discusses the conditions that must be present in an organization to create the types of knowledge that lead to value creation. It provides practical approaches for developing and harvesting knowledge as an organization-wide activity.

Etienne Wenger, Richard A. McDermott, and William Snyder, *Cultivating Communities of Practice* (Boston: Harvard Business School Press, 2002).

This book offers methods and examples of how to develop and support communities of practice that can create, share, and apply knowledge. It also outlines the pitfalls and benefits of such communities.

The Authors

Jeff DeGraff is a member of the faculty at the University of Michigan Business School, where he creates and teaches MBA and Executive Education courses on managing creativity, innovation, and change. He received his doctorate from the University of Wisconsin-Madison. His research and writing focus on innovation and change strategy, innovation incubation processes, developing core competencies for innovation and change, and creative thinking in leadership.

DeGraff serves as an adviser to think tanks, universities, and governments, and he is a popular speaker about creativity and innovation at work. He also works with the investment community in developing effective processes for selecting winning ideas that can be transformed into successful ventures. He has consulted with dozens of the world's most prominent firms and has developed a broad array of methodologies and tools that are used worldwide. DeGraff has worked in more than thirty countries in diverse industry segments including financial services, health care, media and information services, manufacturing, pharmaceuticals, hospitality, insurance, utilities, government, life sciences, nonprofits, and several high-tech sectors.

DeGraff is co-creator of *Wholonics,* a turnkey system for measuring, creating, and predicting corporate performance and value. In the 1980s, before joining the University of Michigan Business School faculty, DeGraff was an executive at Domino's Pizza while it was one of the world's fastest-growing companies. He can be contacted through the book's Web site, www.creativity-at-work.com.

Katherine A. Lawrence is currently completing a Ph.D. in organizational behavior at the University of Michigan Business School. She received a BA from Yale University, a master's degree in educational technology from the Harvard Graduate School of Education, and a master's in psychology from the University of Michigan.

Lawrence's work experiences have ranged from the visual and performing arts to educational media to management research. Early in her career, she did graphic and theatrical design. In London, England, she managed the production of wildlife documentaries that were broadcast on The Discovery Channel and the PBS *Nature* series. Later she worked as an educational technology designer and developer, and then joined Harvard Business School as a research associate, writing cases and other teaching materials.

At the University of Michigan Business School, Lawrence enjoys collaborating on both research and teaching. Her collaborative research has examined topics such as creativity, change, managerial initiative, leadership behavior, and distributed sensemaking. Some of this research has been published in *Academy of Management Journal* and *Organization Science.* Her personal research interests include improvisation, communities of practice, organizational culture, and individual interpersonal abilities, particularly as these relate to creativity. She is also an active member of the qualitative research community at the University of Michigan, supporting the growth of several interdisciplinary initiatives to educate and connect researchers who use qualitative research methods. Her e-mail address is kal@aya.yale.edu.

Index